My Horse Riding Makeover

10 Simple Equestrian Lessons, Habits and Exercises you need to know to improve your horseback riding today

Elaine Heney

Table of Contents

Foreword by Steve Halfpenny

This book is a must-read for anyone who is serious about their horse's well-being and their own horsemanship.

There are many things to consider on the road to True Unity[1] with a horse! The horse's physical and mental well-being are most important, as is good saddle fit for the horse and the rider. Along with the rider's posture and thought processes, this will give the rider a better connection with their horse.

This book covers some of the most important things to consider for keeping your horse sound and the keys for a better connection with your horse. I have known Elaine for quite some time now and she is a great student of good horsemanship. This book is testament to what she has learned on her horsemanship journey.

Steve Halfpenny, Light Hands Equitation.

www.stevehalfpenny.com

---

[1] True Unity is a book written by Bill Dorrance and Leslie Desmond, published in 1987.

Introduction by the author

Last summer I was fortunate to get several lessons from horsemen and women who have an extraordinary understanding of horses. They travelled from the USA and Australia to Ireland to share their knowledge and experience with a small group of riders. They also inspired me to begin a significant horsemanship journey that I wanted to share with you.

At the first clinic, I had volunteered to be the first to ride as the guinea pig, to help the other riders feel more comfortable. So, armed with a ton of nerves and a list of 20 things I wanted to improve with my horse, I rode into the arena. My horse was also feeling very emotional and unsure, so we made an 'interesting' sight!

During that session I learned that the way my horse feels is more important than trying to do various manoeuvres.

When we walked into the arena, I should have thrown away my 20-point list, and simply asked for help to get my horse to feel better.

Sometimes trying to get everything done and tick all our boxes isn't what our horses need.

I like to get things done on schedule and I like to see progress. But it's not the best idea with my horse, and probably most horses, regardless of how many people are watching at the time. I learned that I needed to slow down and listen to my horse more.

During my second clinic, as we worked on groundwork and timing, the instructor demonstrated through her interactions with my horse, that patience, kindness, and simple step-by-step little tasks make it very easy for my horse to learn. Lots of little mental rests and rewards really helped and removed any pressure from the situation.

Even though we were working on fixing a few issues, it was a lot of fun for all of us, including my horse! This calm, thoughtful, unhurried, and happy approach struck a chord with both my horse and me and got wonderful results.

During my third clinic, my trainer from Australia showed me how amazing my horse is. The lesson started out as normal. Then my trainer mentioned my horse was running away in walk. That confused me quite a lot - I had no idea this was possible! We were just walking!

It turned out my trainer was right. Ozzie was mentally leaving and was not with me. Physically, my horse was leaning a little on my hands and wasn't soft. So we worked on it and Ozzie changed once I became aware of the issue and experimented with some ways to change Ozzie's ideas.

As a result my horse got soft. I picked up the reins at halt and had my horse soften his whole body. He was goose-bumps soft!

When we moved I felt my horse, Ozzie, connecting back to me mentally, being with me in every step. This blew my mind. There was no weight in my hands. My horse was weightless and we were mentally together and in balance. I'd ridden for over 25 years and only felt this once or twice before, either on a world-class schoolmaster or just a glimpse in the past with Oz. But never this much or this awesome with my own lovely Connemara.

It was one of those moments that touches your heart and you end up trying not to shed a tear of happiness!

This wasn't the end. With this new softness and connection, my trainer helped us with some more advanced lateral and straight work. Ozzie blew me away. I realised that when my horse was relaxed and comfortable, soft and collected, we could do some amazing things together.

It turned out I hadn't taught Ozzie these things. He already knew how to do these advanced flatwork and dressage manoeuvres! It turned out that while I had been trying hard for us both to improve, it was me who needed the education, not him.

Based on the assumption I wanted to improve myself as a rider - and I wanted to do it before I was 80 years old - I realised that, to get different results, I needed to start doing things differently.

This book is the result of my quest to improve myself as a horse rider. I booked flights and flew to Germany to learn about saddle fit from the general manager of Stübben, one of the most successful saddle companies in the world. I emailed nearly every saddle fitter in the USA and Ireland for help and advice.

I interviewed top international trainers from Europe, Australia, New Zealand, and the USA. I got comfortable and more balanced in rocket yoga lessons, enjoyed Pilates lessons, felt the burn in boot camp sessions, and realised my left knee did funny things when I turned left in Alexander technique sessions.

Along with some amazing friends I laughed, was challenged, improved my fitness (walking over 332,047 steps / 262 km in one month), and had a lot of fun. I learned that daily physical activity can help prevent arthritis, cancer, and depression. I learned about the unwanted results you get if your saddle fits your horse but doesn't fit you. I learned how much more effective it is to think toes up rather than heels down. And I learned how our small daily choices can have major impacts (good and bad) on our lives and our horse riding.

This isn't a book about horses. This is a book for us - this is a book for the horse riders.

If we are truly honest when we look in the mirror, we will recognise that there are a lot of improvements we can make in our knowledge, habits, and lifestyle - to improve our horse riding for the better.

Our horses are there already.

Thank you for joining me on this journey.

You are in the right place.

ೲೞ

Foreword by the author

Horseback riding requires a perfect synergy of poise, grace, and physical alignment. Common everyday habits, from poor posture to stress, adversely impact your overall performance when you ride your horse. But there are simple changes that you can make, starting today, which can have a big positive effect on your horse riding.

The way we carry our bodies is the key to proper alignment and to our overall emotional well-being. Simple shifts in how we approach everything—how we sit, how we breathe, how we use our eyes—can improve horseback riding and so much more.

My Horse Riding Makeover was created to help you discover how you can isolate your bad habits and transform them into good habits!

You'll discover simple techniques you can start using today to help set you on the right path. You will discover insights and advice from leading international doctors, chiropractors, equine dentists, yoga teachers, horse trainers, and posture experts. You will also access special bonuses - exclusive with this book - that you can download instantly at

http://www.honesthorseriding.com/bonus

- The #1 bestselling book *Ozzie: The Story of a Young Horse*

- The Horse Riding Posture Checklist

- Saddle fit and design interview with #1 international saddle company in Germany

- Video #1 in the Honest Horse Riding Yoga for Horseback Riders program

You can achieve greater health, harmony, and happiness in your life and become the beautiful elegant horse rider that you've dreamed of being.

Today is the perfect day to begin.

༄༅

How to use this book

This book contains 10 chapters. Each chapter is focused on one area of your life and your horse riding. You can complete the chapters in any order. At the end of each chapter are three simple and fun exercises for you to complete:

- Online exercise
- Posture exercise
- Horse riding exercise

Most people will read this book, but won't implement what they have learned in their lives and horsemanship.

Be among the 1% of people who will take action! We all have the potential to be beautiful and thoughtful horse riders. I'd love to hear about your progress in our Honest Horse Riding Facebook group.

I wish you every success. You can do it!

Love,

Elaine Heney

www.honesthorseriding.com

Chapter One:

5 Ways to improve your posture every day

"Work on your own posture daily. It matters to both you and your horse if you both want to keep your balance."

--Lisa Bruin, Horsewoman, U.K.

Horse riding is an art form and a way of life. Is not merely a sport or a way to keep fit.

A few months ago I surveyed horse riders around the world from multiple equestrian disciplines ranging from pleasure riders and hackers to competition riders. Was I the only person who had identified my own bad riding habits? Or were there many more like me who wanted to improve their horse riding? Every horse rider I spoke to admitted that they had bad horse riding habits they wanted to fix. It surprised me that every rider had bad habits! The most common bad habit the riders mentioned was looking down when they rode. Other common bad habits included leaning forward, holding tension in their bodies, not breathing, having straight arms, rounding out of the shoulders, having their heels up, sitting crooked and slouching.

These bad habits sound bad - but for most people, they are absolutely normal. So the question must be asked: why do we have these bad habits?

Bad habits are often learned and ingrained through repetition. But the good news is we can "unlearn" bad habits using simple techniques.

Let's begin with learning how to improve our posture, when we are not with our horses.

Babies have perfect posture

Good posture is not good just for horse-riding. Good posture can make you look taller, more attractive, and graceful, and you will exude confidence. Good posture is eye-catching because it's not very common these days. Taylor Swift is one celebrity with great posture. Can you think of any others? In a research paper I read recently, one common attribute in people who live to over 100 years of age is good posture. Not smoking and staying active were also included.

As babies and toddlers, we all had very good posture. Babies can't use muscles to carry the weight of their head because their muscles are not yet fully developed. Instead, babies automatically sit up with straight vertebrae, which perfectly support the weight of their head.

The human body is designed for movement. It is not designed for the many hours of sitting required for our lifestyles today.

Beginning in their early school days, most people develop bad posture habits from crouching over school desks, slouching at their work desk, or slumping in front of the TV. As adults we wake up, sit down for breakfast, drive to work or sit on a bus or train, sit for up to eight hours at a desk at work, drive home again, sit down for dinner and then sit down to watch TV on the couch.

The average American spends 1,700 hours per year at work and can sit for up to 15.5 hours a day. Over the years, bad posture from sitting can develop into back aches and pains.

Bad posture affects our horse riding in an unhelpful way by creating tension and imbalance in our bodies and in our horses' bodies.

As equine expert Amanda Barton advises, *"It is very hard to succeed with something on a horse for 1 hour a day if we are practicing something totally different for the other 23 hours of the day. If we hold our toothbrush so tight that we get white knuckles, take a hold of the door handle as if it was going to escape and wake the neighbours when we slam the car door then there is a good chance that we are going about our daily life holding more tension in our hand, wrist, lower arm, upper arm, shoulders and back than we need to! It's a great practice to work on softness in all these day-to-day things so that when we go to our horse we have been practicing the softness that we want to bring to our touch and to our rein contact."*

A professional opinion

Peter Bennett, a UK-based family chiropractor, regularly treats patients for back and neck pain, as well as headaches, migraines, hearing problems, digestive problems and other ailments. The first thing he looks at in his patients is poor posture.

Peter explains, *"The most common sign of issues is that their posture is out. We see a lot of office workers because they are at their computer all day and they're in a bad posture all day. We get a lot of people in to us who drive all the time… Sales reps, people like that, because they're in a bad posture continuously for hours at a time."*

The adverse effects of poor posture are compounded over time, often taking years to manifest as serious pain. Peter elaborates, *"The average time frame is about 20 years. The initial injury you won't feel at all. What your body will do is compensate. It's extremely compensating and making the best of the bad job, so it will just compensate and compensate and compensate, and you'll gradually accumulate injuries and scar tissue over a twenty year period."*

Step 1: Body awareness

Your bad posture habits become evident when you ride.

The first step to improving your posture, while riding is to notice what your bad habits are in your everyday life. Do these habits also appear when you ride your horse?

You can start improving your posture today with my Horse Riding Posture Checklist. This in-depth list will help you isolate some of the very common posture issues with which most people struggle. It's located in the bonus section as an instant download: http://www.honesthorseriding.com/bonus

Good posture is not about sticking your chest forward, overarching the small hollow in your lower back, and tilting your chin up. This body posture uses a lot of muscles, and you won't be able to hold that position for very long. It can also compress your vertebrae, a situation that can lead to sore backs, slipped discs, herniated discs, and lower back pain.

There are many other common bad habits as well. The slight "S" curve in our backs turns into a "C" curve when we slouch, which many people often do. This body shape squashes parts of our vertebrae and also makes breathing and digestion more

difficult. As our ribs compress on our internal organs, it causes our hearts to work a little bit harder than usual.

Good posture starts with you noticing how you use your body.

- When you are at your desk or computer, notice how you hold your body:

- Do you lean forwards?

- Do you slump in your chair?

- Are your shoulders tense? Can you relax them?

- How is your breathing?

- Do your neck and head move forwards towards the screen?

- Do you tilt your pelvis forwards, creating a hollow in your lower back?

- Do you sit straight in front of your desk, or are you turned sideways a little?

- Do you look down or look straight ahead at your computer monitor?

- Is your chair seat flat or it is higher at the back, or is it hollow or lower at the back? Hollow chair seats and seats which are lower at the back will encourage you to slump.

Step 2: Proper alignment

Something as simple as standing upright or sitting up straight can make all the difference in the world to our long-term health and well-being.

Your head is about as heavy as a bowling ball. Your body works very well when your head is placed on top of your spine. There is a slight "S" curve in your spine, and your head's weight is supported by your bones, rather than by your muscles. Sometimes our head is leaning ahead, tipped behind, or tilted to the side of our vertebrae, using muscles to help support the weight.

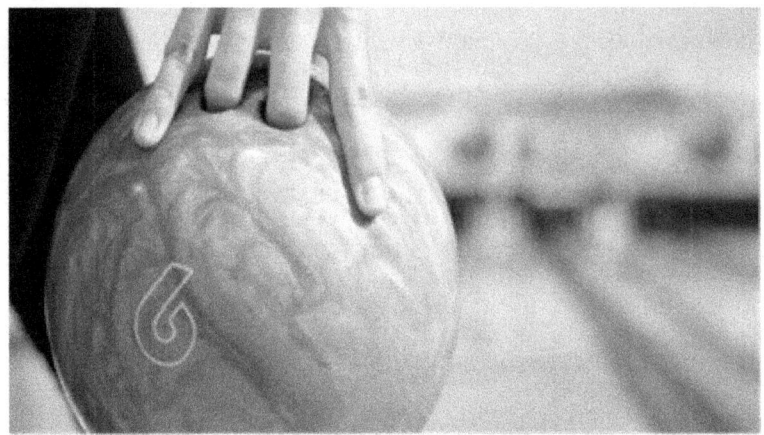

The average adult head weighs 10 to 12 pounds when it's in the upright or neutral position. However, because of that pesky thing called physics—gravitational pull—the cranium becomes heavier the more you bend your neck.

When your head is not stacked on top of your vertebrae, but instead ahead, behind, or to the side, it puts a lot of pressure on our bones and these get squashed or tilted. This position can lead over time to sore backs, slipped discs, herniated discs, lower back pain and other ailments.

The human body was designed to move, not to be still. It wasn't designed to sit for long time periods in chairs. If you work all day sitting down with bad posture, an hour of exercise in the gym each evening will not fix the damage you've done to yourself that day!

Improving alignment starts by standing tall. Standing tall doesn't just make you look better; it optimizes your health too. Studies have found good posture elevates testosterone and serotonin in the body and also reduces levels of the stress hormone cortisol.

Beware of false posture, too; we often think we're standing up straight when we're not. Just seeing yourself in a mirror can help. Mirrors and a helpful friend are great ways to get an honest second opinion.

Step 3: Fixing your work environment

Improving your posture starts with some simple adjustments you can start making immediately, beginning with how you work every day. If you sit at a computer, here is a useful process to follow.

Working At a Computer:

1. Remove your current computer screen from your desk. Close your laptop fully.

2. Look to see if the seat of your chair is flat, tilted back to front, backwards sloping, or rounded or dipped so it looks a little hollow. A chair with a slightly hollow seat or a chair that is tipped back is not good for your back, for it encourages you to slump. A flat chair is fine. A chair with a tilt so the back of the seat is higher than the front will help you to sit correctly. If you have a flat seated chair or a chair that tilts back, you can buy a seat wedge cushion to create this effect. Many people find this cushion useful, both for office work and for driving.

3. Sit on your chair with your hips a little higher than your knees. Your feet should be flat on the ground. If your chair is too high, lower your chair or put a book under your feet, so your feet are resting flat on the book or the ground.

4. Ladies, now is the time to remove your high heels. High heels can cause your pelvis to tilt forward when you are sitting, and your head to tilt backwards too much, putting extra pressure on your back.

5. Arm rests are not necessary.

6. As you sit in the chair, tilt your pelvis forwards and lean forwards. Then tilt your pelvis back and sit on your back jeans pockets. Now adjust your body so your pelvis is pointed straight up to the roof, neither tilted forwards nor backwards.

7. Your keyboard should be at a comfortable height for your hands to use and for your lower arms to rest at.

8. Look forward and imagine a drop of water is running down your nose. The tip of your nose will move down a little as the drop of water runs down your nose. As you do this, your back becomes longer and straighter by itself. Your head is also no longer tilted backwards and instead is supported by your vertebrae, which is now straight. You can play with this position by keeping your pelvis pointed to the roof and nodding your head forwards a few times, until it feels like the weight of your head is at its lightest.

9. Look straight ahead. This is the height your computer monitor needs to be at. Too high and it will cause you to look up and have your head behind your vertebrae. Too low and it will cause you to have your head leaning forwards in front of your vertebrae. If you are using a laptop screen that makes you look down often, it may make sense to invest in a separate monitor that solves this issue. This expense today may save you a lot more money in doctor's fees later in life.

Driving

When we drive, we are also (hopefully!) sitting down. Here are some ways you can improve your posture while you drive, followed by some simple ways you can improve your overall alignment and balance. Before your next drive, look at the seat in your car. Ideally, it should be slightly higher at the back. Or it may be flat. Most commonly, though, it's likely to be lower at the back. This can encourage you to slouch when you drive.

To fix this problem, you can adjust your car seat, or you can buy a firm seat wedge cushion and put it on your seat. If you look at the Amazon reviews, you'll see there are thousands of people who have bad posture habits and back pain, and who have got great benefit from these seat wedge cushions when they drive.

Step 4: Fixing how you sit

Crossing Your Arms and Legs

Crossing the arms and legs is something that many us do, but don't realize it! Crossing your arms can cause you to slouch a little, and it also affects your digestive system. It can put more pressure on your heart and lungs to work properly. If you notice your arms are folded, unfold them and let them hang gently at your side.

Crossing your legs also causes extra muscles in your body to work overtime and increases the tension in your body. Practice sitting down straight without crossing your legs or leaning sideways.

Your Head

Your head and shoulder positions are also very important. With your head weighing as much as a bowling ball, having it tilted backwards too much, forwards too much (like looking at your horses ears!), or sideways on a phone can, over the years, lead to back pain issues when you are older.

If your chin is high, and your head is tipped back, you are putting extra unwanted pressure on your back to hold up the weight of your head. This posture habit is quite common in people and is usually accompanied by an arched lower back as well.

Instead, imagine there is a drop of water slowing running down your nose. Allow your chin to come down a little and the drop of water to fall off the end of your nose.

Step 5: Engaging the pelvis

A very effective way to change your riding position is to become more aware of where your pelvis is pointed. Many women, sometimes because of tight lower back muscles, can tilt their pelvises forwards which causes them to lean forward when they ride.

As you sit (when this habit is more obvious!), put your hand on your lower back, and by moving through a few different lower back positions (leaning forwards/pelvis pointed straight up/slouching) identify when your pelvis is pointed straight up, and practice staying like this in your normal life. The more this becomes a daily habit, the more likely you'll start to do this unconsciously when you ride too.

Practise each day repositioning the pelvis so it points up. Imagine the top of your head touching the sky. By doing this regularly, you'll feel taller, with a flatter stomach and lower back. The upper body becomes more energized and not slouched, reducing the likelihood of lower back pain. This new body habit will also help improve your balance when you ride.

Chapter 1 Assignments

Online exercise

Like the 'Honest Horse Riding' page on Facebook. Stay in touch with an amazing community of people who support your goals. Facebook page:

https://www.facebook.com/honesthorseriding

Posture exercise

Follow the steps in this chapter to improve your posture at your computer by checking if your chair is suitable. Re-adjust the height of your chair and monitor as required. Fixing your posture at your PC will make a BIG difference! You will be able to start to create some new posture habits over the next few weeks.

Riding exercise – part 1

When you go horse riding, while at halt and also in walk, your exercise today is to find out where your pelvis is usually pointed. Different people have different habits. If you are slouching in the saddle it is likely that your pelvis is pointed backwards a little.

If your pelvis is tipped forwards, you will probably have your chin tilted upwards and head back a little behind the balance point.

- To test what habits you have, ask a friend to hold your horse for you at halt, while you sit in the saddle.

- Place one palm on your stomach, and one palm on your lower back.

- Experiment between arching your back, and then slouching while you sit in the saddle.

- Can you find the place in the middle where your lower back feels flat against your palm?

Riding exercise – part 2

Now your pelvis should be pointed straight upwards. The next step is to check if you have a habit of leaning backwards or forwards in the saddle.

- Imagine the top of your head touching the sky.

- When you do this, do you adjust your upper body forwards or backwards?

- You might have to do these two or three times, to become aware of your body moving.

Thinking of your head touching the sky is a great way to check if you are sitting up straight in the saddle.

If you did find that you moved forwards or backwards a little during this second part of the experiment, you probably have a habit of either leaning forwards or backwards a little too much to begin with.

Don't panic. You've actually done something really wonderful! You've started to notice what your habits are.

Habits can be changed, but only if you are aware of them. It's all about awareness. So by improving your awareness with these little experiments, you've actually done more than 50% of the work in this book already! And it's still only chapter 1!

Congratulations!

Now you are ready to complete the Posture Checklist at http://www.honesthorseriding.com/bonus

ಸೋಡ

Chapter Two:

Get fit and healthy

"I absolutely believe that real progress begins with working on the inner horseman—my own experience tells me this is true."

--Tom Widdicombe, Horseman, UK.

Life is hectic. Most of us react by rushing through our days, from task to task. We have so much to do that 24 hours in a day does not seem enough. But rushing causes a lot of tension in our muscles, which can wreak havoc on our bodies.

The issue with tension is that you will lose energy faster than you should, as you are using too many muscles. As a horse rider, tension in your body will often lead to tension in your horse's body, which you absolutely do not want.

The effects of stress on the body

Stress is a very physical event. We feel stress most clearly in our muscles, particularly in the neck, shoulders, back, and face. We even use the words 'stress' and 'tense' interchangeably. 'I feel tense' can often mean the same as 'I feel stressed'. It is easy to see why. The stress response is all about physical activity. Because we now lead such physically inactive lives, we forget how much our bodies and minds are engineered for movement. The stress response has one goal alone - namely purposeful action.

A stress response starts in the brain. Your brain detects a problem and initiates the contraction of big and small muscles throughout the body. This 'coiled spring' feeling is called a 'preparatory set.' The body is setting itself up in preparation for action by tensing the muscles appropriate to that task.

This coiled spring feeling is exactly what a zebra experiences just before it flees from a lion. So why don't zebras get ulcers, like we do? After all, they face lions! And we can get ulcers facing a computer screen!

The answer is simple. The zebra gets to run, and we don't. The zebra breaks out of its preparatory set, and its muscles are freely used for the purpose for which they were designed. They stretch and contract fully and become filled with blood and oxygen.

The zebra's muscles get a few minutes of high quality, life-enhancing exercise that also enables them to return easily to rest afterwards. In contrast, we hardly ever get that opportunity. Because we remain tense, we face a different kind of muscle strain compared to a zebra.

We are like a runner forever at the starting blocks of a race. A runner has to prepare to run and to simultaneously inhibit that impulse until exactly the right moment. If he had to hold that position for minutes, the strain would become unbearable.

This type of strain is called isometric tension. Certain muscles are contracting while opposing muscles also tense up to inhibit their movement. The muscles are burning a huge amount of energy with no visible movement to show for it. This prolonged strain is how we can get very tense and very tired just sitting at a desk. We would use less energy going for a walk.

Stress always involves muscle tension. Fortunately, it is one part of the whole stress dynamic that we can easily do something about and the entire body benefits if we do. If we feel our muscles relaxing, we know we have activated the other aspects of the relaxation response as well.

Because the body is so interconnected, we can be confident that our heart rate, blood pressure, and cortisol secretion will be returning to normal. Digestion and immunity will be able to function well again. Muscle tension is a marker for the whole stress-relaxation dynamic in the body.

Chronic tension

Chronic tension is bad for the body in many ways. Chronically tight muscles can't relax completely, even when they have the opportunity to do so. It is not easy to shift from isometric tension to full relaxation. If you've been tense at a desk all day, your muscles won't relax completely as soon as you lie down in bed. Tight muscles need to be stretched out through activity or exercised to relax well.

Chronic tension doesn't feel good at all, and we start to move cautiously to avoid hurting ourselves, like elderly people do. Occasionally, when you see an older person who has retained the suppleness of youth, you can see proof that a tight, closed-in body is not an inevitable consequence of ageing. It is, however, a very common consequence of ageing.

Muscle pain makes us feel old. Tight muscles don't function well and tend to atrophy. They lose their ability to relax completely. They are like muscular straps that are tightened a little more each year. Worry makes the neck and shoulders tighten, pulling the shoulders forward. By middle age worry can permanently hunch the upper back.

If our muscles have been tight all day long, they will remain partly contracted even in sleep. This means that our sleep can be edgy and disturbed, and we can wake up still feeling tense. Because our mood is our mental interpretation of bodily sensations, this residual tension can make us feel anxious even before the day has begun.

Mindfulness

Managing stress and making positive changes in your life starts by changing the way you approach and view your daily life; your mindset determines your outcomes. When you shift your perceptions to see a bigger picture, positive changes can start to take place.

London-based physician Dr. Nikki Osborne elaborates: *"Mindfulness is a technique that has been developed essentially by psychologists and doctors and is used to manage stress and anxiety and depression, often for patients who are suffering for those problems. But really, it can be used for all of us in dealing with our daily life stresses. Our minds are something that happens; we are not our minds. The faults that come to us that just appear in our heads are not necessarily correct. They're not necessarily appropriate judgment."*

Negative thoughts can lead to stress, anxiety and fear, but by seeing them for what they are—just thoughts—we can neutralize them. Dr. Osborne explains, *"They're just thoughts that are popping into our mind and they may or may not be helpful. So taking time to practice this when anxiety and faults pop into our mind, just to take a moment to step back, notice them and actually not resist them but actually release them and let them go again is not necessarily correct. It's just things that are popping into our mind. It sort of removes the power of them and the ability for them to inflict the anxiety on us. It gives us back a little control".*

Meditation and reflection, two other major components of mindfulness, also come into play. Dr. Osborne suggests, *"The key aspect of mindfulness is being present in the moment and meditation. Mindfulness involves meditation, but essentially what we're doing is meditating on the present moment, and often it's on the breath, just a nice and easy thing to focus on. So it's just about taking a few minutes and something you need to learn to do basically, it's not something that comes naturally to us. Take a few moments, sit calmly with a nice, relaxed but upright position away from the back of the chair, ideally not lying down or anything and just sitting calmly and upright, feet flat on the ground and you're taking the moment to just focus on your breath that goes in and goes out. You're not trying to change anything. You're just being aware of it."*

Cultivating mindfulness

- When you rush, you tense up and lose the softness in your body and your body retains more tension. When you walk, practise strolling slowly and don't walk really fast. When you need to go faster than a stroll, jog or run instead of doing a fast walk. We weren't designed to do those fast little tense walks!

- You can practise becoming more aware by taking 10 steps. During each step, notice the feeling you get in each foot as it meets the ground. Does your heel touch the ground first? Or does the ball of your foot touch the ground first? Does your left foot meet the ground in the same way as your right foot does? Do you have a habit of taking your first step with your left foot or with your right foot?

- When we rush around all day, we carry that tension in our bodies. We clench our asses. Our shoulders are up around our ears and our arms and hands are tight. But rushing is not something that has to happen. We have the power to choose not to rush. Life is not an emergency. We can choose whether we will allow a situation to cause us stress. Sometimes, something as simple as a mindset change can really impact your life (and your horse riding) in a huge way.

- Here is a nice way you can evaluate if something is worth getting stressed over. In a year's time, will you still remember what you're currently about to stress over? If the answer is no, then it's a very good reason not to get stressed.

- Imagine you are late for a flight and sitting in heavy traffic five miles away. This is another situation when it's not worth getting stressed because you do not have the power to change the situation. Getting stressed is a waste of energy.

- For everything that happens in your life from today onwards, imagine you have three options: you can do what you normally do, you can do something different, or you can choose to do nothing. Doing nothing is often the best option!

By slowing down, choosing not to get stressed, and doing more of 'nothing,' you can arrive at the stable yard energized and refreshed, rather than stressed and tight. You may notice you will feel a lot happier and more relaxed as well.

Body tension—Life is not an emergency

Being stressed can cause physical changes in our bodies and minds.

We can feel like we are under pressure. Our breathing can become fast and shallow. Stress can cause us to worry about the past or the future and stop us from living in the present. Physically, stress can result in tension being held in our bodies. Tight shoulders. Clenched glutes (buttock muscles). You can't concentrate, and you find it hard to relax physically. We can have low energy and tense muscles and be disorganized and forgetful. None of these things are good for our horse riding. It's worth noting that anxiety and stress can lead to heart problems and strokes, which we absolutely do not want.

Now, let's look at what not being stressed looks like.

Your muscles are relaxed. Your glutes are not clenched tight and your shoulders are relaxed and not near your ears. You are feeling calm. You're living in the moment and feeling happy. Your breathing is slower, and you find it easier to concentrate and deal with life. Perhaps you are smiling.

We all have trigger points that cause us to get stressed. Our trigger points may be someone at work, being late for a meeting, or any one of a million little things that can overwhelm us when we are feeling under pressure.

But nearly everything can be changed or adapted.

First, life is not an emergency. We can choose whether we will allow a situation to cause us stress. Doing things quickly is ok, but doing things while hurrying and tense is not so good.

Imagine you have an 8 a.m. meeting. What can you do to reduce possible stress? You can prepare in advance. You can set two alarm clocks to go off a little early, to give you extra time to get to the meeting so you will not have to rush in the morning. Instead when you're queuing for a Starbucks, you can be kind and allow the really stressed out person to skip in front if it means that much to them. Upon receiving an award for the most beautiful woman in the world, Sandra Bullock said beauty is not what you look like. Beauty is based on the kind and thoughtful actions you do each day for the people, animals and environment that you encounter.

Now imagine you woke up late for the meeting.

You have two options:

Panic, stress, dash to the meeting and be late anyway.

Or you can send a message to your workplace, apologize for running late but something personal came up. Then without stress or rushing, go through the process of getting to work. Yes, you'll be late, but you'll still be calm, relaxed, and feeling much healthier.

In your daily life, choose not to rush so much anymore. Stroll when you walk. Enjoy each moment. Life is short so treasure it.

Yoga for horse riders

Another effective method to reduce body tension and practice mindfulness is by doing yoga and pilates.

Yoga, in the simplest definition, means "unity." Yoga postures, also called "asanas," help strengthen the body and physical coordination to become more physically fit. Yoga requires concentration, self-control, self-power, and self-discipline. Yoga works toward self-awareness of the body, mind, and spirit, both separately and in their unity with the ultimate object of finding peace and serenity within, regardless of outside circumstances

Yoga poses take very little time to do. Most postures take only a minute or less and are done as a series, incorporating several postures in each part of a class flow. The series of flowing movements generate heat, allowing the body to stretch deeply to increase flexibility. The breath work (or "prana", meaning "life force") required throughout the workout focuses the mind, increases awareness, and reduces stress. The result is a vigorous, cardiovascular fitness experience that simultaneously strengthens the body, mind, and spirit. The relaxing and meditative practice allows for a calm and focused mind. Focusing on good breathing techniques while moving your body at the same time is wonderful practice for horse riding.

Regular yoga and pilates practice improves suppleness, balance, relaxation, and breathing awareness. Yoga and pilates can make you feel happier and more confident and help you to sleep better.

As part of this book, you can watch the first video in our Yoga for Horse Riders program at http://www.honesthorseriding.com/bonus.

This yoga program was designed by Elaine Heney in partnership with a remarkable Indian yoga instructor and is specifically tailored for horse riders looking to improve their balance, suppleness, and posture.

Yoga can help you change your body, inside and out. Preeti, our Honest Horse Riding in-house yoga instructor who hails from Rishikesh, India (the birthplace of yoga), explains: *"The benefits of yoga start when you start the stretching and the breathing techniques or the meditations. You feel the strengths of your body, changing your body language."*

Yoga can make you more flexible, have more stamina, and reduces stress. Having a regular yoga practice promotes peace of mind, improves focus and concentration, increases your lung capacity and metabolism, and helps digestion. It can improve your physical coordination and balance, lead to better muscle tone and strength and increased body awareness and it can help you to feel good.

A really good way to get started is to join a local yoga or Pilates class. If you don't have enough time, or there are no classes near you, there are many other options.

There are also many different yoga and pilates apps available for both Apple and Android platforms. You can use these at a time that suits you. Even just 10-15 minutes a day will really change the way you feel.

YouTube is also a great resource. Not only does it have millions of cat videos, you'll also find some great yoga and pilates lessons there that you can work on at home.

It really is amazing how you can feel your body becoming more relaxed and supple after a few weeks.

When you get started on your own yoga journey, don't forget to access your exclusive 'Yoga For Horseback Riders' video we've created just for you at http://www.honesthorseriding.com/bonus

It is part of the special bonuses you get with this book. Make yoga or Pilates a small part of your day for the next two weeks. You'll be amazed at the changes it can bring to your life.

ഇരു

Chapter 2 assignments

Online exercise

Watch video #1 in our Honest Horse Riding Yoga for Horse Riders series here at http://www.honesthorseriding.com/bonus This will take approximately 10 minutes to complete.

Posture exercise

Notice three times this week when you are rushing at home or at work. Each time, make a mental decision to relax and slow down. Notice how this mental decision makes you feel, physically and emotionally.

For 10 steps, either in shoes or barefoot, focus on feeling each foot as it touches the ground gently.

Riding exercise

This week, for the 60 minutes before you ride your horse, I want you to focus on relaxing your shoulders, breathing out deeply and not rushing. The goal is to arrive at your yard relaxed, smiling, and feeling happy. Your mental and physical state can have a major impact on the quality of your session with your horse.

Chapter Three:

Breathing and smiling

Breathing

Breathing is something that we as humans have to do to stay alive! But often we hold tension in our lower backs. This tension, along with other factors, can make our breathing shallow and not as effective as it could be.

If you've watched showjumpers exiting an arena after a round, or if you've ever ended up out of breath while jumping or getting a lesson, you will recognize that horse riders can also STOP breathing in times of pressure or stress, when they are riding their horse. Not breathing for certain periods of time is not good for our bodies. The resulting tension in our bodies is evident to our horses and is likely to influence their behavior and movement as well.

In our daily lives, bad posture makes it harder to breathe properly and puts extra stress on our lungs.

But there is good news: you can fix your breathing and start to wake up your diaphragm again. Using your diaphragm will naturally improve your posture and help your horse riding!

Posture and breath

Let's test out how breathing can help you to sit or stand taller.

Sit on a chair with your two feet flat on the ground. Now gently lean forward and put your head between your knees, and look at the ground. Become aware of your breathing. Breathe in and out with slow deep breaths. As you breathe in, notice how your lungs expand and your body wants to get a little straighter. Allow your breath to move your body so it lifts up a little.

By doing this technique for about half a minute to a minute, your natural breathing will push your body up a little each time until you are sitting upright again.

In reality, to sit or stand up straight you don't have to make your body do anything. You just have to allow your breathing to move your body back into its natural position.

There are different ways that people can breathe. We are looking for the most effective and simplest way, using the least amount of muscles possible.

Sometimes, people breathe and their shoulders rise up a lot, or they expand the front of their chest a lot. What we really want is for you to engage your diaphragm muscles, which are located underneath your rib cage. When your diaphragm muscles rise, they squeeze your lungs and you blow out air. When they lower, they make your lungs bigger, and you breathe in air.

Practice for a few minutes thinking 'down' when you breathe in because when you breathe in, your diaphragm is going down!

Many of us have forgotten that we need our diaphragm to power our breathing and we should reduce shallow breathing from the top of our lungs. There's a really simple way that you can start to improve on how you breathe.

First up, breathe in and then breathe out.

After your breath out, pause, with no air in your lungs.

Stay like this for as long as you can. It may be a few seconds, or it may be 10 seconds or longer.

When your reflexes kick in, and you take your next breath, your diaphragm will actually be working! This method of breathing is wonderful because your moving diaphragm will help you breathe efficiently and deeply. Your moving diaphragm will also result in your Psoas illacus muscle group relaxing as well (these are the muscles in your ass), which will directly relate to relaxing your leg and thighs when you ride.

Practice this 'pause' after your breath out at least 10 times every day. You can do it anywhere - when you're walking, at your desk in the office, wherever suits you best.

Breathing while you ride makes a huge difference to your horse's movement and stops you from getting red-faced and out of breath too!

Breathing using your diaphragm when you ride is really good for your lower back muscles. It will also help you to have more relaxed legs and glutes and to be able to feel your horse's movements much more easily. This method of breathing will be a huge benefit when you are getting more advanced and need to be aware of when each of your horse's feet are moving.

Proper breathing also impacts your horse as well. As International Horsemanship trainer and instructor Lisa Bruin advises, *"Breathe deeply and calmly, so your horse can move freely and smoothly."*

Breathing is also essential to your riding practice.

Horseman Ben Moxon elaborates, *"I learned years ago about the value of exhaling through a transition. It doesn't matter whether you are speeding up or slowing down, it always takes energy for your horse to make that change and exhaling helps that stay smooth. You can reach a point where you can simply breathe and make a transition without needing more obvious cues."*

Smiling and facial relaxation

We can hold a lot of tension in our faces and around our mouths. Oftentimes, we are unaware that our lips are tight. Tight lips can cause the muscles in the back of our neck to be tight as well. Tension in our lips and face will then affect our whole back area, causing unwanted tension.

It's really useful to become aware of this held tension in lots of different situations. Do you tighten your mouth when you are at a computer? When you go for a walk? When you are watching the TV? The first step is to become aware of when you hold tension in your body.

The second step is to relax and separate your lips. A great way to do this is by smiling!

When your mouth relaxes, it will actually encourage the muscles around the back of your head to relax as well, which is great to encourage softness in your body and release tension.

It's a very good idea to smile when you are riding. Happy rider, happy horse! Use trigger thoughts – a happy horse moment, something you are proud of about yourself, or a funny moment you shared with another person. Also, you'll be amazed how much better you'll look in photos! A smiling rider is always a great sight to see.

Start practicing by noticing when your lips are tight and then allowing a slight smile to play at the edges of your lips when you are at work or walking around town. You'll feel more relaxed and you might just make some other people smile too.

The Alexander Technique

A couple of years ago, I stumbled upon a unique approach to transforming bad habits—and getting great horse riding photos—called the Alexander Technique. A fellow writer and friend of mine in England always had the most amazing photographs taken of her. I was curious to know her secret.

As a rider, you have to get accustomed to people taking photos of you. Sometimes they can be really nice, and sometimes they can be not so nice! But in every single photo of my friend riding, she was just beautiful. Her photos look effortless and incredibly eye-catching. When I asked her how she was able to produce such flawless photos, she mentioned that she had studied the Alexander Technique.

Maria O'Neill, a much sought-after Alexander Technique teacher in Kildare, Ireland, explains the technique simply: *"The Alexander Technique is about changing the bad habits* that we all have. Whether it's when we are writing or sitting at computer, or walking down the street or dancing, or whatever we do. The technique was developed by a Tasmanian actor and horse rider named Alexander, who suffered from throat problems that impacted his acting abilities."

Maria continues, "Doctors told him there was nothing wrong, so he eventually decided that it was something he was doing to himself. He looked at himself in the mirror for seven years and worked out he was actually causing the problem to himself with his tension. So that's basically where the technique evolves from. So he realized that he could break his bad habits by becoming aware of them and actually direct himself into new action, new activity which would correct the problems that he was having."

The Alexander Technique can help the horse rider greatly, starting with posture. Maria explains, "A lot of our stress is held in the shoulders, and of course, that's neck related. When we talk about riding, any habits that we have when we're sitting, standing, walking, talking, we bring into our riding. That is why, as an Alexander Technique teacher, I work with many riders including professional horse riders. Sometimes just noticing will resolve an issue, sometimes they *have to change and do something totally different. The issues we have when we ride horses are really the same issues we have when we're walking and doing all the normal daily things that we do."*

Improving posture isn't solved by sitting up straight. Sitting up unnaturally straight can introduce tension into the body. *"That's the problem with people when they're told, as we are growing up, to stand up straight, sit up straight,"* Maria says. *"The problem is we bring more tension into the equation. So rather than actually doing something, what we've got to do is undo the tension. We need to undo the habits that we have created over our life to hold us up or to do the things we do. The idea of standing up straight and holding yourself up straight only gets us into more trouble and does us more damage. The premise by which Alexander works by releasing tension is allowing your whole body to lengthen and soften and allowing your postural system which we override all the time. The basic idea is that we're holding ourselves up at the back. If you think of your back as one big long muscle, you're holding yourself up with that long muscle at the back. It's better, in terms of standing up straight or sitting straight on a chair, to think about releasing, allowing your back to lengthen and soften; allowing your head to release away from the top of your spine; allowing your nose to tilt gently, softly towards your chest and allowing yourself to sit down into a chair."*

What about our natural tendency to slouch? The Alexander Technique proposes an alternate approach, as Maria explains: *"Because we slouch and because we're so oriented towards the front of our body we use a lot of tension and we use a lot of work using our hands, using our legs and using our reflexes all the time. Allow the body to release down into a chair, with your feet placed squarely in front of you so that you're making good contact with the ground, especially when you're sitting at a computer or you're working, that you have that stable base underneath you. So it's really about releasing your way to the floor."*

Improving our breathing can have a hugely positive impact on our horse riding. *"We really need to keep breathing because that helps to keep the tension out of our bodies,"* Maria concludes. *"Remembering to breathe, and noticing yourself when you're not breathing, is really, really helpful."*

꧁꧂

Chapter 3 assignments

Online exercise

Download the My Horse Riding Makeover App. Because I get great value from listening to podcasts and audio when I am jogging, hiking, and driving my car, I've created an iPhone and iPad app where you can listen to the exercises from this book. It's called 'My Horse Riding Makeover.' You can download it from the app store here:

https://itunes.apple.com/app/my-horse-riding-makeover-free/id931210201?ls=1&mt=8

Posture exercise

Re-engage your diaphragm when you breathe. First up, breathe in, and then breathe out. After you breathe out, now pause, with no air in your lungs. Stay without breathing for as long as you can. It may be a few seconds or it may be 10 seconds or longer. When your reflexes kick in and you take your next breath, you will be using your diaphragm. Repeat this exercise for one minute every day.

Riding Exercise 1: Observation

While riding your horse in a walk, start to notice how you are breathing. Are you breathing quickly or allowing your diaphragm to engage your breaths? How many breaths do you take in one lap of your paddock or arena? Now, do a small and simple exercise with your horse. This exercise can be anything from a turn or serpentine to a walk – trot – walk transition. Did your breathing get faster? Can you do this small exercise while also focusing on your breathing at the same time?

Riding Exercise 2: Enjoy a 'Breath-Through!

For a few minutes while you ride or handle your horse, breathe in and out slowly, deeply and loudly, so that both you and your horse can hear your breaths. Notice if this helps to relax your horse. Does his release any tension in his body? Does he lower his head a little, bebd a little better, yawn, or lick and chew more than normal?

ஐ൬

Chapter Four:

Your 15 minute posture transformation

You can positively impact your tension, posture, and stress levels.

This is a 15 minute posture and rebalancing exercise that you can do to relax your body, realign your vertebrae and de-stress. I find this exercise really effective to do just before I ride my horse, especially if I've just spent a few hours hunched over a computer.

Posture transformation exercise

- To start this rebalancing exercise, you'll need a quiet room, and you will lie down on a yoga mat or on the carpet where you are comfortable.

- Have a paperback book handy, and put it under the back of your head, so your head can rest comfortably on it.

- Lie down flat on your back, looking up at the ceiling.

- Now, gently bend one knee and slide that foot up so it's close to your backside, but not touching it.

- Now gently bend your other knee and slide your other foot up towards your backside.

- Your two feet should be about shoulder-width apart and flat on the ground.

- Next, put a little weight into your feet so it feels like your spine is being pushed away from your feet and your back is getting a little longer.

- You want to make sure your lower back is flat against the floor. You can put your hand at your lower back to check your lower back is flat. If you need to, reposition your feet with your knees still bent and your feet on the ground so your lower back is touching the floor. This technique is really good to correct any slouching or tight back muscles you were using during the day.

- Finally, rest your fingers gently on your hips and allow your shoulders to widen and your elbows to lie on the ground a good distance from your body.

- This posture relaxes your upper body, and the stress you are holding in your shoulders will start to fade away.

- Stay in this posture for 10 to 20 minutes and enjoy this moment of peace and quiet.

- This is a really good exercise to do once each day.

Learning how to relax your body helps you greatly when riding. As the incredible German horse rider and trainer Isabell Brenner explains, *"I move with the horse so I don't do any movement on my own. I just sit, relax, and let the horse move my body. All I do is try to sit straight and stay balanced and relaxed and just let the horse move me."*

Learning how to relax isn't just important for you—it's also important for your horse.

Isabell elaborates: *"The more relaxed you are, the better you can feel the horse. The more relaxed you are, the more relaxed the horse will be. If the horse is relaxed, it moves more freely. If the horse gets tight, it doesn't move as freely and then it makes it harder to feel the horse's legs move, you can't feel the timing as well."*

In our quest to be good riders, it is quite common to try too hard, and this usually does not help us to reach our goal. The stillness that you can see in wonderful riders comes from movement with the horse. This is possible as the rider's body is relaxed and then it's easy for the horse's movement to influence the rider's body. The result of this is seeing both horse and rider moving as if they are one entity, rather than two separate beings. If you try too hard to hold a posture or try to be still, you will probably be holding tension in your body. This will jar with your horse's movement and make it harder for both of you to be moving in harmony together.

As you ride, start to notice which areas of your body are tense and relax them. Can you notice how your horse moves your body in walk?

Relaxing the body requires you to relax the mind as well. And how do you relax the mind? Live in the moment and be present.

One amazing part of being a horseman or horsewoman is being around these incredible creatures every day. Because horses naturally live in the moment, I find spending time with my horse helps me to find a better connection to the world and to the present. I have a wonderful grey Connemara called Ozzie with whom I've had many adventures.

If you are interested in learning about how I bought and worked with a pretty determined and opinionated horse and all of the highs and lows that go with horse training, you can download the digital copy of my bestselling book, *Ozzie: The Story of a Young Horse* here:

http://www.honesthorseriding.com/bonus

ഌ‍ൟ

Chapter 4 assignments

Online Exercise

Download the *'Ozzie: The Story of a Young Horse'* book here: http://www.honesthorseriding.com/bonus

Posture exercise

Find a quiet space where you won't be interrupted and complete the posture exercise above 3 times this week.

Riding exercise

While riding your horse at a walk, think about what Isabell said:

"I move with the horse so I don't do any movement of my own. I just sit, relax, and let the horse move my body. All I do is try to sit straight and stay balanced and relaxed and just let the horse move me."

When you ride, can you find what areas are tense and relax them one by one? Can you focus on not doing any extra movements and feel what it's like to allow only the horse to move your body? How little can you move in the saddle?

This focus can cover everything from nagging with your legs and overusing your hands, to tensing your body unnecessarily and clenching your legs and your ass. It's a really interesting exercise to focus on, and the results can be phenomenal!

It's important to realize you don't have to be perfect right away. By starting to become aware of your habits, fixing them becomes a lot easier with a little relaxation practice.

ℰⓒℬ

Chapter Five:

4 Proven happiness hacks

The 2012 best-selling book, *Finding a Future That Fits,* by famed life coach Louise Presley-Turner, takes an interesting approach to helping people find true happiness.

The book asked the readers a few questions to see if they were happy with their lives. What are your answers?

- Do you wish every day of the week away? When it is Monday, do you wish it were Tuesday? When it is Tuesday, do you wish it were Friday?

- Do you watch far too much TV or spend too much time gossiping with friends or on social networks?

- When you get together with your friends, do you all moan about how hard your lives are?

- Do you blame a bad upbringing, lack of education, the economy or other factors? Do you feel like a victim?

- Do you envy people who seem more successful than you and resent them?

- Do you drink, smoke, or shop too much as a way to feel better?

- Do you catch colds or get ill a lot?

There are lots of other questions and interesting ideas that Presley-Turner delves into, but these were the ones that really struck a chord with me.

Most people want to be happy. A very good way to be happy is to do things that you are good at and you like to do.

I was guilty of the first two questions. Every Monday I wished it were Tuesday, and when the winter arrived and the evenings got dark, I watched way too much reality TV.

I was pretty good at my job as a software manager in the city, but I wasn't enjoying it anymore. I was lurching from crisis to crisis, and while each project turned out fine in the end, the process wasn't something I was enjoying much. Twelve hours at an office desk isn't good for anyone.

With my head so full of work stuff, to relax each evening I turned on some bubblegum TV, as my brain had no more capacity at that time to deal with new or more interesting things. I was on the verge of a burnout.

But there are things we can do to take control of our lives. No one is actually a victim. It might be as simple as talking to your boss, letting him or her know you are overloaded or that you'd prefer to spend more time in a different area of the company which fascinates you. One lady spoke to her boss about what skills she would really like to focus on, and she went from being a stressed out bunny to helping the company out with several new designs and graphic promo materials for a new campaign they were launching. She was much happier as a result.

I went a bit more extreme and realized that the only way I could ride my horse every day—which definitely makes me very happy—was to quit my job and start my own business. So I decided to try that. It was an experiment.

Life hack one: isolate your areas of unhappiness and create a plan

Ask yourself what areas of your life are making you unhappy.

Here is a list you can run through:

- Your relationships

- Your work and career

- Your personal image

- Your health

- Your finances

- Your view of the world

What are the two areas in your life with which you have the biggest difficulties?

What advice would you give to yourself to fix these two areas?

Oftentimes, we know the answers already, but we may not have actively thought about them properly before. There are options in every situation.

I learned a really interesting angle on happiness from hip-hop mogul Russell Simmons. He believes that the actual work you do in life is the source from which true happiness will stem. If you put your heart and soul into what you do, the outcome will naturally take care of itself. This belief applies really well to horsemanship. Horse riding is not really about winning rosettes against your colleagues to boost your ego or passing exams judged by someone else. Horsemanship is about putting your whole heart into every moment you share with your horse every single day and enjoying the fulfillment it brings to your life.

Life hack two: the happiness technique

When we get to the yard, it would be great if we felt happy. In fact, in life in general, happiness is what a lot of us are looking for.

I recently listened to a good iTunes podcast which you can also listen to in the bonuses area. It proposed that the reason we don't feel happy is because we compare ourselves to others who are—or who appear thanks to social media!—more accomplished, smarter, and more talented than we are ourselves. I've definitely been guilty of comparing myself to others in the past.

Instead, what we need to do is to stop comparing ourselves to these type of 'over-achievers' (or maybe just good self-promoters!). If you must compare yourself, compare yourself to where you were a year ago and look at all of the progress you have made. It's a really interesting concept and worth listening to.

I played the piano in school and college. I would get lost for hours in Beethoven, Ravel, Chopin and Debussy, my four favorite composers. I didn't play because I had to for my college exams. I played because I loved to play. Once a year, I sat an exam, and while getting the piece of paper to say I passed was fine, it didn't mean as much to me as the rush I got from actually playing the music each day. I loved what I did; the outcome wasn't as important. Because I loved what I did and thus got pretty good at it, the outcome took care of itself.

In the same way, I started doing some new horsemanship exams in my twenties. For a year or two, I got a great buzz out of getting a new horsemanship certificate to hang on my wall. I was really getting somewhere with all these bits of paper on my walls! Then I bought a horse that taught me that there was only ever one judge I needed to focus on, and that was him.

I realized then that the buzz I got from connecting with my horse, seeing our improvements, and having him as my sole judge was a million times more rewarding to me than a piece of paper. I stopped doing horse exams and allowed my horse to teach me directly. As a by-product of letting my horse's progress and needs guide me rather than trying to please an examiner, I'm sure I'm now a lot better in my horsemanship than when I was mainly focused on ticking off boxes on a test sheet.

Don't get obsessed with your achievements. This could include getting more collection, more impulsion or getting a better circle. If we pressure ourselves too much we can take the joy out of riding. We ride because we love horses, and riding horses makes us feel happy. If you are not happy with your progress or your horse's progress, then it is probably worth taking a look to see if the path you are on is the right path for you today. Don't be afraid to take the pressure off and go back to focusing on having fun and learning interesting things again. There are lots of incredible horsemanship teachers who can help you along and lots of new friends waiting to meet you!

I believe horsemanship is not about focusing hard on the end result. It's not about rosettes or exams. It's about putting your whole heart into every moment you share with your horse. My main goal with my horse is to help him feel comfortable and happy. If I can do that then everything else, whether it's a soft side-pass or a beautiful balanced bend, is so much easier.

Life hack three: the compliment method

This is a nice way to hack happiness. It's my quick fix, and it just takes a few seconds. Walk up to someone and pay him or her unexpected compliment. It can be something as simple as 'I like your shoes' to 'you're looking marvellous today!'. Who doesn't like to be told they look great?

One thing to never do (and I have no idea why people do this) is to tell people that they look a bit tired, fatigued, or run down. Instead, find one thing to compliment and just say it. I guarantee if you say something complimentary instead of something that could be perceived as critical, both of you will be smiling.

Life hack four: pause to think

"Life is 10% what happens to you and 90% how you react to it."

--Charles Swindoll

We don't always have to react when something happens, but automatic reactions in certain situations are habits that a lot of us do. We react first; sometimes we also get emotional, and we think later.

There's a small technique that has changed people's lives for the better. It has transformed stressed-out, angry people into calm, relaxed versions of themselves. It involves pausing and then choosing to do one of three things.

As you become more aware of what you do, you can decide to stay as you are, doing something different, or to do nothing. Just thinking about what you are going to do for a second before you start to do it can make a huge difference.

Think about getting up from your seat. When I am aware I am about to get up, I think for a second and decide to get up in a way that doesn't strain my lower back.

Just like everyone out there, I am human. Sometimes I forget!

Once, in a fitness boot camp in Ireland, we were all sitting down for a rest. I got up without thinking about it, and got up in a way that wasn't kind to my back. Then I realized what I had just done.

So I sat down again and got up again, slowly and properly, in order to practice a new habit. Most people don't know what's happening around them because their minds are elsewhere and not in the moment. There was, therefore, a pretty good chance no one even noticed that I got up off the chair twice.

Think about being cut off in traffic. You can do what you normally do which may be to beep your horn, shake your fist, or get all tense and wound up. It won't help the situation as you've still been cut off.

You do something different: you can turn up the radio, grumble under your breath and so forth, which doesn't involve creating as much tension.

Or you can get cut off, and you can choose to do nothing. You will get the same result, but you don't get stressed, you don't feel that build-up of tension in your body, and you don't let it affect your mood. Maybe that driver is trying to get to the hospital. Maybe it's a learner driver. Maybe it's an older driver who is feeling pressured. Maybe it's a driver who got very little sleep last night and is on edge.

Maybe it's not always about you. Choosing to do nothing can enrich your life significantly.

Keeping track

Keeping a journal is a great tool for self-improvement. Whether it's a bound notebook, a Word document or an online journal or blog, writing down your progress and your observations can help you isolate areas of improvement. Many of my friends do this and tell me it is invaluable! It doesn't have to be long, and can take just five minutes after you ride each day.

You can even create your own book at the end of the year and celebrate how far you've come!

ᎮᏃᏆᏃ

Chapter 5 assignments

Online exercise

A happy rider makes life so much easier for your horse! Your challenge this week is to pay someone an unexpected compliment every day.

Posture exercise

Not enjoying our lives can impact our posture and general health a lot. This week I want you to identify one area of your life you'd like to improve and to implement one small thing to make a change.

Riding exercise

When you are riding your horse this week, start to become aware of how you instinctively react in normal/common situations, often without thinking. Then I want you to pick three times this week when rather than doing what you normally do, instead pause, think, and either:

1. Do something different from normal;
2. Do nothing and wait.

I find that doing nothing can be really interesting with horses. Sometimes, the best thing to do is to give your horse more time. Of course though, if your horse spooks or you need to stop him as there's a train coming, then get effective immediately! Safety always comes first.

ജൗങ്ങ

Chapter Six:

Saddle and stirrup designs that work

Your riding posture and how you sit in the saddle is influenced by the design of the saddle you are sitting on. You could have beautiful posture, but sitting in a saddle that doesn't fit you or your horse correctly can leave you looking ungraceful and impact your ability to be in balance with your horse.

Let's look at why you need the saddle to fit your horse correctly, and then we will investigate how to find a saddle that fits your body as well.

A friend of mine wisely wrote on Facebook a few weeks ago:

"Anyone who doesn't believe saddle fit is pivotal to both the horse and rider should be made to spend a few hours in a pair of thick wool socks, shoved into a pair of stiletto pumps two sizes too small... and then they must balance themselves AND carry a couple of heavy squirming humans for good measure."

I think many riders get a saddle fitter out only to check their saddle if they have reason to believe the saddle may be not fitting correctly or causing their horse pain in some way. Many times, if they don't detect any obvious discomfort from their horse, the saddle doesn't get checked for years, maybe decades.

Common problems that your saddle can have include the following:

- The saddle is too narrow and is sitting too high on your horse's back and may be pinching.

- The saddle is too wide and is sitting too low on your horse's back and not offering enough protection to his vertebrae.

- The balance point of the saddle if too far back and is making you look like you're sitting in an armchair. Significantly, this can also put the rider's weight further back on the horse's back, where it is not as strong. This is a very fast way for your horse to get a sore back. A lot of saddles have this issue.

- The flocking in the saddle has gotten old and thin or perhaps is now unbalanced and needs to be reflocked.

- The saddle is bridging. Underneath where you sit in the saddle is not touching the horse's back. This bridging can cause pressure points on your horse's back and soreness and white hairs if not fixed quickly.

- The saddle is too long. If your saddle is too long for your horse and extends past the end of your horse's ribs, then your saddle will be putting weight on an area of your horse's back that is not suitable to bear this type of weight. The long saddle length can cause tight muscles underneath the back of the saddle and can translate into back pain for your horse.

This is a quick way to get your horse checked: contact an equine physiotherapist and ask them to visit your horse. This should be done once a year anyway. They will check your horse's body and tell you if there is pain in any area, which you might be currently unaware of. If your horse is sore:

1) You want to know about it immediately. No one wants their horse to be in pain.

2) This pain can be affecting your performance. Circles might not be quite as good as you want on one rein, or your horse might not have as much impulsion as you want. Both of these issues can be caused by a saddle that is too narrow.

3) If you keep ignoring it, you might end up in getting into trouble some day when your horse can't tolerate the pain any longer. Some horses can go for months or years in pain and not show any obvious signs to the rider.

These are all great reasons to get an equine therapist to come and visit you to check your horse's body. If you live far away, why not get a few friends together and make it a fun social day?

Saddle fit

Saddle fit is hugely important for all riders to get right in order to have a horse that is pain free and able to perform all of the physical movements you would like without restriction. Correct saddle fit is not a 'nice to have', it's actually a 'must have'.

The saddle has to do many jobs, and it must fit both you and your horse. Given all of the different shapes we come in, finding a saddle that is balanced and fits you both can mean you need to try out a lot of saddles to find the one that's perfect for you both. It also doesn't mean your new saddle has got to be the most expensive saddle or the current brand name in vogue; instead, it must be well made and suitable for you and your horse.

To get answers to my questions, I flew to Germany to meet Johannes Stübben, the general manager of the Stübben saddle brand, and spent seven hours at his workshops outside Dusseldorf learning how Stübben designed and fitted their saddles. You can check out my interview with Johannes Stübben online here:

http://www.honesthorseriding.com/bonus

It was fascinating to see every stage of how saddles are made, including a room with a full wall of trees waiting to be used.

Stübben explained, *"If the rider or the owner of the saddle treats the saddle well, the product can last at least for the horse's life, maybe longer. Picking the right saddle is key—we have hundreds of different models, including 50-60 regular models, each with a variety of different lengths and block sizes. It's hard for the rider to pick correct saddles alone, so they need instruction on how to pick the best possible fit."*

Good fit starts with balance. Stübben elaborated: *"Balance is probably the most magical word in the riding industry. Maybe the back of the saddle is too low, maybe the tree is improperly placed. Finding the right balance is the most important thing to experience good riding."*

Here are some things to check and see if the saddle fits your horse:

- Each day before you ride, run you hand along your horse's back slowly and check to see if there is any tightness or soreness anywhere, which might provide a clue that your saddle is causing an issue. You can do this as follows:

- Ask your horse to stand quietly at halt. When he is relaxed and standing still on a loose rein (so he has room to move if he wants to), imagine dividing the area where the saddle will be into three different sections – front, middle and back.

- Rub your horse's back in the 'back' section, where the cantle of the saddle would be. Does he stand still or start to walk?

- Rub your horse's back in the 'middle' section, where the rider would sit on his back. Does he stand still or start to walk?

- Rub your horse's back in the 'front' section, near the withers and top of his shoulders, where the front of the saddle would be. Does he stand still or start to walk?

- If your horse tenses up or starts to walk when you rub one area, but not the others, it could be quite likely that the saddle is making him sore in that area. I would get an equine physiotherapist out to check and confirm immediately.

- If your horse unexpectedly stops moving or behaves in a different way one day, saddle fit is always something I check. Maybe the saddle is pinching, maybe the flocking has got thin, maybe the saddle is old and worn out (as happened to my old saddle, and my horse refused to walk forwards one day!), or maybe there is a nail or something odd that's now coming through the flocking and hurting your horse.

- Saddles should be checked once a year, as the flocking will compact and may need to be adjusted. If your saddle hasn't been checked in over 12 months, your action item this week is to find a saddle fitter and get him or her out to visit. If they live far away, then get a few of your friends together and get him to visit with all of you together for the day.

- You don't need a very expensive saddle, but you definitely should not ride in a very cheap saddle. At Stübben, we saw how they designed and made their saddle tree. Johannes showed us how the tree can bend from side to side when he twists it and also how it moves when there's pressure put on the seat area. It's got flexibility. This is something that cheaper saddles (I'm thinking saddles that are made in Asia and cost about $100) are unlikely to have. Cheaper saddles may also be made of materials like PVC or something similar that do not allow the saddle to move very much as your horse's body moves, and so will restrict your horse's movement. Leather is a natural material which will move with your horse's movements a little. If you have a non-leather saddle, it may be perfectly fine but I always suggest researching the material and its performance against the traditional leather. What are its advantages and disadvantages? You can Google this or ask an independent saddle maker. Sometimes it can be difficult to get a completely un-biased answer from the person who is looking to sell you a saddle (either for or against it, depending on what they are selling!).

- Another interesting point is the length of the saddle. Saddles which extend past the horse's 18th vertebrae, after the ribs end, put pressure on an area of the horse's back which is weaker. At a clinic, one horse was wearing quite a long western saddle. When the horse's back was checked, the muscles just under the back of the saddle were tight. While it wasn't causing pain right then, it could lead to a back issue in the future for that horse. You do not want your saddle to be longer than it should be.

- Run your hands over your horse's back, where the cantle/ end of the saddle would be if you have not already done this earlier in this chapter. Check if any muscles are tight here or if your horse starts to walk or look uncomfortable. To find out where your horse's ribs end, ask your vet when he visits next while your horse is wearing a saddle. If your saddle touches your back behind this area it is not good for your horse. Your saddle does not fit. When Isabell Brenner came to visit, I asked her to show me exactly where the last rib on my horse was. I compared this area to something visible on Ozzie's body. So now I can tell the exact place the ribs end on my horse's body from looking at his hair pattern.

- According to Johannes Stübben, each saddle needs to be balanced. It should not be tipped backwards or tipped forwards. If the lowest point of the saddle is not in the middle of the saddle when you put it on your horse's back, then that saddle simply is not balanced and doesn't fit your horse. Padding, shims and other similar supports will not fix this. They will just put pressure on other areas and your saddle still won't fit properly. It's also worth noting that the saddle may be fine; it just may not suit the shape of your horse's back. A lot of saddles, especially GP and jumping saddles, can have large leg rolls which both make the rider feel more secure in the saddle and push the seat of the saddle backwards a little on the horse. This can put the rider's weight too far back on an area of the horse's back that is not very strong, and can cause back pain for your horse.

- When you are buying a new or second-hand saddle, try at least 15 to 30 different saddles on your horse before you find 'the one'. And it will still probably need slight adjusting. It takes a while to find a great saddle that fits, but it is worth the effort for years to come. To do this, you'll need four things in the same place: you, your horse, a GREAT saddle fitter, and some saddles to try. Looking at a shiny saddle at a show and deciding to buy it without trying it on your horse with a good saddle fitter present is NOT a good idea.

Check out my interview with Johannes Stübben online here for more insights: http://www.honesthorseriding.com/bonus

Saddle fitters

Like all professions, you can find great saddle fitters who are worth their weight in gold to check your saddle fits and is comfortable on your horse. I've even heard stories of them helping out when a brand new saddle arrives and there is a fault with it and they can check this, and the saddle may even need to be sent back to the factory where it came from. A great saddle fitter can make sure there are no fit issues and help your horse to feel great with maximum movement when you ride him. It's worth getting your saddle checked each year as horses can change shape over time, and also to check if the flocking needs to be revisited, as it can compact over time.

Like most professions, you can also get saddle fitters who are not worth paying any money for! I have just finished a horse clinic where all six horses had saddles that didn't fit correctly and were hurting their horses. This clinic was with riders who really wanted to make sure their horses were comfortable and unfortunately trusted three local saddler fitters who confirmed that these saddles fit! None of the six riders could use their saddles any more. It was an absolute nightmare and the equine physiotherapist had to visit two of the horses the next day. To read more about our saddle fit disaster, and to find out some ways that can help you find a good saddle fitter, visit: http://irishhorsemanship.com/4-simple-questions-to-use-to-find-a-good-saddle-fitter-and-how-to-avoid-the-many-bad-saddle-fitters-out-there.

When choosing a saddle fitter, I would always advise calling (by phone) at least five saddle fitters (even if they do not live nearby). Calling by phone is preferable to email. With a 1-1 chat you can get a much better idea of their quality. Aim to ask them the questions in the blog post above. Then only invite the one saddle fitter who has the most knowledge on the subject to visit your horse.

Saddle and stirrup design

Your stirrups can make a big difference to your riding as well. I really like forward-facing stirrups. They make a huge difference when getting up from block, regaining your stirrup after you lose it, and feeling more secure in rising trot.

Saddle and stirrup position

- Stirrup position should be at the acupuncture point in your foot, not at your toes, just behind the ball of your heels. This stirrup position is a great way to improve the 'lower leg moving' issue.

- When your stirrups are near your toes, when you trot, your lower leg can move forward.

- When your stirrups are back a little, when you trot, your lower leg is likely to move less.

- Don't squeeze or tighten your toes.

Bits

In Germany, I heard a story about a horse that was bought in the US for €30,000, and brought to Europe. Then someone put a €30 bit in its mouth with no thought about whether it fit the horse or not.

You need to study the horse's mouth before you choose the correct bit. Knowing the form and shape of your horse's mouth is critical to choosing a bit which will be comfortable for him.

Check bars of the mouth. This is the area between the front and back teeth. It is skin on bone. Are there any weird things growing there? Any bumps? Smooth bars are very good.

Check your horse's mouth's width, which is different on every horse.

Your horse's tongue can be thick, normal or thin and sit below the teeth. This detail makes a huge difference concerning what bit will fit. If your horse's tongue is very thick and the roof of his mouth is very low, you do not want to put a very thick bit into his mouth, for there will be literally very little room.

How low/high is the roof of your horse's mouth? Is it deep or shallow?

Because we're not always used to looking at horses' mouths, a great place to start this research is by asking your horse dentist on their next visit, to tell you what type of mouth your horse has and what size and thickness of bit they think suitable.

How bits fit is an essential part of maintaining optimal equine dental health.

A bit that doesn't fit your horse, or is causing pain, can often result in your horse needing to open his mouth, or move his head in ways that are not usual. Any head shaking or excessive mouth and lip movements while riding should include a thorough investigation of your horse's mouth and teeth (perhaps there is soreness somewhere which your equine vet can check for you), and the suitability of his bit for his mouth shape and size.

As equine dentist Maria O'Rourke elaborates: *"A correctly fitting bit is very important not only because it is the communication between the horse and rider but also to ensure comfort and avoid injuries to the mouth. The most common areas are the tongue, palate, soft tissue area in front of the first premolars and the bars (the space between the front and back teeth where the bit lies). Unfortunately, horses tend to push into pain possibly evading the bit or ignoring it completely which may result in the horse becoming very strong, shaking its head or refusing to turn. This can result in attempts to gain respect/control by changing to increasingly severe bits causing more and more pain to the horse and possible desensitisation of the mouth and hence no communication between horse and rider. Horses' mouths vary in size and shape and it also changes shape throughout the horse's life, so a bit that fit perfectly well as a five year old may not fit the same horse 10 or 15 years later."*

Nosebands

Over the last 20 years, a fashion has emerged of strapping a horse's mouth shut with various nosebands including flashes and grackles. It is quite common now to see these at horse shows and equestrian events. Any time a horse is exhibiting unusual behavior - excessive mouth opening, etc, there is a reason behind it. It is generally wise to investigate what is causing the issue. In many causes, ignoring the cause and focusing on minimising the symptoms (such as with the use of nosebands that strap the horse's mouth shut) may not be in the best interest of your horse's health or your riding quality.

Bill Dorrance explains this in more depth in his book 'True Horsemanship Through Feel'.

'Most horses will close their mouths naturally when the bit is adjusted low enough to allow for that. With a calm mouth like the kind I'm thinking of, why I doubt there'd be any need to buckle his mouth shut. To close off his natural jaw movements produces tightness all through the horse..... [the whole mouth area is] one of the most sensitive places on a horse.'

'If a horse isn't able to move his jaws or breathe freely for any reason, well, just about all of his movements are going to be compromised. Under circumstances like this, he's also affected mentally.'

If your horse shows issues with his mouth, and you may have gone down the road to tie his mouth shut in some manner, then it's a good time to get your equine dentist out for a visit to see if they can help to advise you on what may be causing this in your horse's mouth. It may be as simple as changing your bit.

ಬೂಛ

Chapter 6 assignments

Online exercise 1

Watch these 9 short videos on about good saddle fit: http://www.honesthorseriding.com/saddle-fit/

Online exercise 2

Open up your computer and pull up Google. Type in 'equine physio' and your local area. Get an equine physiotherapist out in the next two weeks to check your horse for any pain or stiffness.

Online exercise 3

Read my blog about our saddle fit disaster and find out some ways that can help you find a good saddle fitter here: http://irishhorsemanship.com/4-simple-questions-to-use-to-find-a-good-saddle-fitter-and-how-to-avoid-the-many-bad-saddle-fitters-out-there/

Posture exercise

Find a friend with a camera. Sit on your horse at halt and think about the top of your head touching the sky. Then look straight ahead, smile, and ask your friend to take a picture of you.

What you're looking for is that there is an imaginary line running from your shoulder to your hip to your heel. Don't panic. From what I've seen, a lot of people look a little more like they are sitting in an armchair. So your legs are out in front of you, and if the horse were to disappear, you would probably end up on your ass on the ground.

This armchair style seat can be an indication that the saddle may not be in balance on the horse's back. It is sitting you too far back and putting weight on an area of your horse's back which is not that strong. This can lead to pain for your horse and an equine physiotherapist visit! When you look at a saddle on a horse, the lowest part of the saddle should be in the middle of the seat, not near the back of the saddle.

Horse exercise 1

- Ask your horse to stand quietly at halt beside you in a halter, while you are on the ground. When he is relaxed and standing still on a loose rein (so he has room to move if he wants to), imagine dividing the area where the saddle will be into three different sections – front, middle and back.

- Rub your horse's back in the 'back' section, where the cantle of the saddle would be. Does he stand still or start to walk?

- Rub your horse's back in the 'middle' section, where the rider would sit on his back. Does he stand still or start to walk?

- Rub your horse's back in the 'front' section, near the withers and top of his shoulders, where the front of the saddle would be. Does he stand still or start to walk?

- If your horse consistently starts to move when you rub one area, but not the others, it could be quite likely that the saddle is making him sore in that area. I would get an equine physio out to check and confirm immediately.

Horse exercise 2

- When your vet visits next, or when you are at a horse event where you can talk to a vet, while your horse is saddled ask the vet to show you where your horse's ribs end.

Horse exercise 3

- If your horse opens his mouth a lot when you use the bit while riding, get an equine dentist out to visit and help you to figure out the cause of this behaviour.

Riding exercise

Sit on your horse and try your stirrups in these two positions: at the ball of your foot and also a little further back. At halt, stand up and sit down a few times in your stirrups. Get someone else to watch you and notice what results you get for both stirrup positions. Does your lower leg move more in one position compared to the other?

80CB

Chapter 7:

Stop staring at your horse's ears

Looking down is the most common habit that horse riders want to fix. Looking down changes the balance of the head and puts the head a little in front of its naturally balanced position.

Looking down can cause a rider to tip forwards more than necessary. By looking down, the weight of our heads pulls us down; therefore, the front of our bodies compresses and our backs over-extend. We are out of balance, and our muscles are working harder than normal to keep us upright.

Looking down unbalances us, makes the horse's job more difficult, and makes us more likely to fall off. It also changes the balance of the head and puts the head a little in front of its natural balanced position.

When we look down, we're compromising alignment, and without proper alignment, our lives are out of balance, inside and out.

Alignment, simply put, is when the vertebrae stack one on top of the other from the base of the skull to the tip of the spine.

The head sits on a joint called the Atlanto-occipital joint. Optimal alignment occurs when the head is lightly poised atop this particular joint.

When we look down, in riding or in any other aspect of our lives, we're putting pressure on the Atlanto-occipital joint. Remember, as we covered in Chapter One, the average adult head weighs 10 to 12 pounds when it's in the upright or neutral position. When you look down, you're adding up to 12 pounds of pressure to the joint and, concurrently, to your entire spinal column.

When we're properly aligned, our heads move in a natural forward position. When we look down, however, the weight starts to compress the joint, putting more strain on your upper back and shoulders.

Adding 12 pounds of pressure is enough to throw off anyone's balance, including your horse. Our vertebrae are incredibly flexible, allowing us to bend and flex in different directions, and when we're properly aligned, we can stretch and even lengthen muscle and connective tissue.

Looking down also makes it hard to see where we're going. Kas Fitzpatrick, founder of Exploring Horsemanship, explains why: *"The human head typically constitutes about 8% of our total body weight, which is a lot really when you think about it. If we look down when riding, say at our horse's ears, we're loading that 8% on to their forehand, not to mention the fact that we're probably tipping a bit more of our body weight in that direction as well. It makes a lot more sense to be looking in the direction we are going, and if we don't do that then we'll never reach the nirvana of being able to have our horses react to subtle changes in our body and energy rather than pressure on the reins. If you also have a tendency to look at the ground all I can remind you is that, really, you need to look where you are going. In case of a spook, you just don't need to have already tipped a larger percentage of your weight downwards."*

Why do we spend so much time looking down?

People look down for any number of reasons. Maybe they're shy, maybe it's just an old habit they've had for years. Whatever the justification, the behavior can have serious consequences, not only for our riding, but for our physical health and wellbeing.

Thankfully, this very common habit can be improved.

Simple exercises to retrain your vision

Here is a really effective exercise to focus you on where you are going, rather than looking down when you ride. It's called the 'Eyes First' method. You can begin by practicing this for a few minutes right now, while you are sitting on a chair or at your computer:

- Begin by standing still and looking straight ahead.

- Now move your eyes only (and not your head!) to the right.

- Now move your head to the right.

- Now move your eyes back to the middle.

- Now move your head back to the middle.

- Now move your eyes to the left.

- Now move your head to the left.

- Now move your eyes back to the middle.

- Now move your head back to the middle.

- The rule here is to move your eyes first to where you want to go and then to move your head and body afterwards. Your eyes move first.

Once you get used to this technique, practice using your 'eyes first, then turn' while walking around your kitchen, while you jog, while you are walking to work, or while you're walking around the supermarket.

Then while you walk your horse in a safe arena, paddock, or field, practice this as well. Move your eyes to where you want to turn to, and then move your head. Do lots of turns and serpentines using this 'eyes first' method.

Another method is by changing how we use our eyes.

Peripheral vision is key to maintaining proper eye direction, however we frequently act as though we have blinders on, only focusing in one direction. As Amanda Barton elaborated: *"Sometimes riders find it hard to avoid staring at their horse's ears, even if their trainer constantly asks them to look up, because they have a habit of using their eyes with a narrow, hard focus called tunnel vision. It is often helpful to change the way that we are using the eyes, rather than just trying to alter the head position. If we can relax the eyes to allow them to take a wider, softer focus called peripheral vision then not only can we see a great deal more of what is going on, be a little more sympathetic to the near 350 degree vision of a horse but also it becomes easier to breathe and to still the mind."*

Use your peripheral vision to avert your eyes from the horizon line. This way, you can see what's all around you without throwing off your balance and adding unnecessary stress to your spine. As you ride your horse in a straight line in walk, check how far you can see to your right and left. Can you see more on one side than the other?

Then as you continue to ride in walk on a straight line looking ahead, start to become aware of how much of your horse's ears and head you can see, while still looking straight ahead. It may be more than you had expected!

The going underfoot

When we are concerned about the going underfoot, it is understandable that we look down to check it out. What we can try is to look a little further out and use your peripheral vision to scan the ground closer to you but without dropping the head down too much or just looking at the ground immediately in front of the feet. Our peripheral vision is amazing, and we can actually see a lot more than we realize, so look a little further out and use the eyes rather than dropping the head right down.

Unfortunately, our balance is compromised by looking down at the ground right in front of our feet, and we are more likely to fall, for the head is already taking us downwards. By looking a little further out and using our eyes more to scan the ground rather than dropping our heads down, we can be more poised and in essence be more able to right ourselves if we do have a little trip.

Leaning forwards when you ride

Another reason many riders look down is that they lean forward. Leaning forward when you ride can be caused by a few issues.

If you are feeling nervous and tense, you will often tend to go into a mild fetal-like posture in the saddle. You'll crouch over and tip forward a little. Another reason for leaning forward a little could be the design of the seat of your saddle. However, a very common cause of leaning forwards when you ride, especially for women, is the position of your pelvis.

- Do not move your body.
- Put your hands on your hips.
- Is your pelvis tilted forwards?
- Is it pointed straight up at the roof?
- Are you slouching, and is your pelvis leaning back?

What we do in everyday life often shows up when we ride.

The next time you are in the saddle and standing still, notice how your pelvis is tilted. If it is tilted forwards or backwards, readjust it so it is now pointing to the roof. Notice how the change in your pelvic position changes your upper body position. Does it decrease your leaning?

Can you start to become more aware of your pelvis position when you are sitting at a desk or a table and check now and again that it's pointed upwards? How many steps in walk and trot can you take without going back to your old habits?

Can you become more aware of your pelvis position when you ride and also check now and again that it's pointed upwards? You'll get bonus points if you can relax your shoulders each time you point your pelvis to the roof.

Don't forget to breathe.

We've discussed the importance of proper breathing already, but it's important to revisit it when discussing posture during riding.

Bad posture makes it harder for you to breathe properly and puts extra stress on your lungs. Breathing naturally will help your posture.

The easy saddle exercise you can do at home

I recently received a newsletter in my email from one of my favorite horse trainers, Steve Halfpenny.

It read:

"Quite a few years ago, while attending a Buck Brannaman clinic, Buck made a comment at the end of the session that really stuck in my mind. He remembered most of the people riding from a previous clinic that I also attended and he said, "Most of you riders have not made many changes in the last 10 years." Although I was only a spectator at this clinic, it had a profound impact on me. I thought to myself at the time that if I ride with Buck, the next time he saw me ride, he would definitely see that I had improved!"

It was with that mindset that I came up with what turned out to be a very effective plan. I could ride my horse for only a limited number of hours each week, for I had to work as well. I needed to think of a way to practice my riding position while I was using my computer.

At home, I decided to change the chair I use at my computer. I took away my current chair and replaced it with a stool. On top of the stool I put a rolled up yoga mat and a cushion, and on top of these, I balanced my saddle. Then I put a long mirror beside my new 'saddle chair' and sat on the saddle chair to do all of my computer work.

What I now had was about two more hours every day in the saddle and at any time I could glance to my left and see what my position was like. Was I slouching? Was I tipped forwards? Were my glutes relaxed? Was I tensing my thighs?

The indoor saddle chair experiment turned out to be really useful. I had a habit of leaning forwards and clenching my glutes. Every time I glanced in the mirror while I worked, it reminded me to relax and reposition my upper body so I was sitting up tall again.

You can use my own Horse Riding Posture Checklist to fine-tune your posture, starting today. It's available for you in the bonus area at http://www.honesthorseriding.com/bonus.

ೞಚಚ

Chapter 7 assignments

Online exercise

Download and complete the Horse Riding Posture Checklist from this web site: http://www.honesthorseriding.com/bonus

Posture exercise

Create a chair for your home computer out of a stool, your saddle, and a few cushions. Put a long mirror right beside it, so when you sit on the saddle, you can see your reflection and posture in the mirror. When you are at your computer this week, glance over every now and again, check your posture and adjust it as needed.

Riding exercise

When you are walking, think about turning your eyes before you turn your head. Practice lots of circles and serpentines.

ᏸᏣ

Chapter Eight:

Get out of your horse's way

"Horses are like a mirror to your inner feeling, they will do what you do, feel, and show up your habits. You can make your horse more worried, braced and reactive, or more relaxed. It's your choice."

--Cathy Johns, New Zealand.

As horse riders, you've probably sat spooks a few times in your life. Animals seem to have an ability to go from seemingly relaxed to 'sudden energy' in the blink of an eye when something frightens them.

As humans, we don't have a lot of natural predators to fear in this world, so there could be an argument made that our bodies have become complacent. If something was to frighten us, we often don't have that immediate split-second, high energy response.

If you analyze this reaction further, the human can actually switch off their body muscles. Think about leaning against a wall. A lot of your muscles aren't working anymore; instead, you're using the wall to hold you up. If a lion jumped out, you'd be in trouble because it'd take a second or two to energize those muscles again and get them moving. Unfortunately, by that stage, you're probably dead meat. We also switch off our muscles as well when we go from a walk to standing still. This can result in a hollow lower back, pelvis forward, and head a little back. Sometimes our upper body can even be switched off while we walk. This posture habit can cause us to drag our heels.

Animals don't tend to switch off their muscles. To survive, they have to be mentally and physically ready to move very quickly. This includes when they are relaxing or doing low energy work.

What would happen if you kept your body energized all of the time?

Exercise: Walk a few steps and then gently stop, but imagine you are about to start walking again. While your feet physically stop moving, the inside of your body is still thinking of moving ahead again. All your muscles are energized.

Like horses and other animals, your body should always be ready to go somewhere. Don't switch off and dump your weight on the floor. Your whole body should feel active even when you are not moving. You should feel like you are about to move.

Pause to think

Imagine a spectrum where one end is calm and worry-free, and the other is emotional and worrying. Each day, your horse will be somewhere on this spectrum, and the exact position usually changes each day. Sometimes they feel greater confidence and are relaxed. Other days, they are a little more on edge and emotional.

I ride a horse who moves between calm and a little emotional, based on various factors. You can read about our journey at: http://www.honesthorseriding.com/bonus

One of these factors is me. While we are riding, if I am asking for a lot of really focused, precise work, it can lead to a little emotion in my horse. I find a little emotion leads to softer and lighter work, but too much emotion can lead to worry and reactions and bracing. My horse's emotional state is always changing, so after some more demanding focused work and a little rise in his emotional level, he takes a rest on a long rein for a minute or two, releases his emotions, and comes back to being calmer and worry free. I do need a little emotion, for being too calm and worry free can translate into being lethargic and sleepy. If I am the cause of my horse's emotion, I can remove or reduce the stimulus and moderate his emotional levels.

Now consider a horse that has become emotional or worried or stressed because of an external factor: a deadly 'rock' in a field, high winds and noise, or fresh cattle running about in the field next door. Your horse is likely to deal with his emotions by using his feet; he will trot, gallop, buck, and move about until he has mentally come to terms with the situation through using movement as his path.

As humans, we can operate in a very similar way. When we become stressed, if we can remove the cause (a friend that really isn't doing you any favors, a job you hate, etc.), we can reduce our stress levels.

If we can't remove the cause, then like horses out in windy noisy weather, we have to deal with the results somehow.

Staying stressed in that situation for long periods of time is not a good idea. Like horses, we too use exercise to reduce our stress levels and allow our mind to work through the situation while we move. You've probably heard of people who need to go for their daily run or workout session to calm themselves down and get rid of tension. It's very similar to how horses cope and it works really well. If you are feeling stressed, and you can't remove the cause for now, a great way to deal with it is to start moving, doing any form of exercise you want from a walk to a yoga class, a game of golf, and beyond.

Another thing to be aware of is your stress threshold. Each individual will have a different stress threshold. What is stressful for one person will not be stressful for another.

We covered the topic of stress earlier in Chapter 2 and how most things in life are probably not worth getting stressed over.

Now, let's look at how stress can impact your horse.

Pause to think about your horse

Anxiety and stress are dangerous for you and your horse. Tension in your body is likely to lead to tension in your horse's body.

We can choose not to feel stressed—to be nonreactive—and feel happier, healthier, and more balanced.

With horses, we also tend to fall into the "react first think later" pattern. The really good horseman you come across will often tell you to do less, and you'll get more. They will also explain to you the value of not rushing, and of setting things up and waiting, letting something happen, and not making something happen.

The next time you ride your horse, when something happens, first pause and think. Remember there is no rush. Then decide if it makes more sense to react as you normally do, to do something different, or to do nothing at all. A lot of times with horses, doing nothing is actually the right option.

Visualization

Visualization is a really powerful tool that riders of any level can use to improve their horse riding.

Years ago, there was a pilot captured in Vietnam. He spent five years there in solitary confinement. He played nine holes of golf every day in his head while he was in prison. He felt the grass under foot and imagined every single moment of playing golf. A few years later, he was released from prison and he travelled home. The first time he played golf after he was released, he got his highest score ever, and he continued to play at that level.

When I am out walking, I've started to imagine I'm actually riding my horse. I make sure my pelvis is tilted upwards. Then I allow the top of my head to touch the sky each time I breathe in. I ask my shoulders to relax, and I practise turning with my eyes first and then my head. Lastly, I relax my mouth and allow a smile to play on my lips. It really is amazing the difference practising this method can make to you. I now start to do some of these things unconsciously when I go out for a walk and when I ride, which is exactly the progress that is really beneficial to you as a rider.

Another very interesting way to apply visualization is to do the following:

Think back to a wonderful ride you had on your horse that made you feel really happy. Write it down as specifically as you can. Relive the moment and relive how it made you feel. Now think of an object to represent this feeling... a star, a diamond, a flower, or anything that speaks best to you. When you sit on your horse for 30 seconds, stay at halt for a while and think about this object and the feeling that goes with it.

Clenching your glutes while riding

Clenching your gluteus maximus muscles—aka the "glutes" or buttocks muscles—is quite common in horse riding, and this continous clenching has a huge and negative impact on your riding.

If you clench your glutes, your body will get pushed out of the saddle a little.

This glute clenching leads to more tension in other areas of your body. It causes tension in your legs and stops them moving as freely as they should.

126

Glute clenching is likely to impact your breathing, for it can stop your diaphragm from moving freely, so your breathing can become shallower.

It also stops you from feeling your horse's back and leg movements, which are so critical, as you need to know which legs are moving when so that you are in time to cue the correct foot for transitions and lateral work.

How do we fix clenched glutes? We notice that they're clenched, and then we invite them to unclench. Oftentimes, in a few seconds, they may just clench up again. That's not a problem. When we notice this, we just allow them to release again and repeat as often as necessary.

You can practise this at work, on the bus, when you walk, in the shops, anywhere. There is no need to carry all of this extra tension in your glutes.

Riding exercise:

- Sit on your horse. Are your glutes clenched? Invite them to relax.

- Walk your horse. Are your glutes clenched? Invite them to relax.

- When you do lateral work, do your glutes clench? Invite them to relax.

When you unclench, you'll feel your horse's ribs a lot more. You'll also be able to move your legs much more independently.

When you do a sitting trot, you'll be able to sit much more easily with unclenched glutes. You'll find your horse feels a lot softer, and you'll get a slower more relaxed and suppler trot. You feel like you are floating!

To help to improve this while you ride, every time you breathe out when you are in the saddle, imagine the air going straight down out of your glutes to the ground. This technique helps to both relax your glutes and improve your breathing.

Relax your thighs

Riding exercise: Now that you are working on relaxing your glutes, the next exercise is to relax your thigh muscles and your knees which may be clenched.

You don't want to clench your stomach, or hold in your stomach because that tension will also affect your pelvis area. This will restrict pelvic movement when you ride and cause tension in your upper legs. Any extra tension in your body will impede your riding.

Your pelvis

Many women tend to push their pelvis forwards because of a tight lower back.

You need to loosen the lower back and to get the pelvis back to being straight up. You can achieve this by engaging your diaphragm.

You can also practise walking and sitting while thinking about having your pelvis pointed upwards. I myself do this on long walks and find it really effective. In fact, when my pelvis is pointed upwards, instead of forwards, it looks like I have a really flat stomach (though I'm not holding it in!), and I can feel my abdominal muscles working on their own. Amazing!

If you're trying to get a flat belly by doing lots of push-ups without engaging the pelvis, you're not going to get results with a pelvis that's tilted forward and a tight lower back. Relax your back and adjust your pelvis for a flatter belly.

Your fitness

We can't expect our horses to be the epitome of equine fitness and health if we drag ourselves around like a sack of potatoes and don't exercise our own bodies. Horse riding is a 50/50 partnership. Honest horse riding is about acknowledging this fact. It's very important, both for our health and for our horse riding progress, that we exercise on a regular basis, ideally every day.

The world-famous Mayo Clinic in the US has made the following recommendations for your weekly exercise:

"150 minutes of moderate aerobic activity a week. That's 25 minutes a day. This could include brisk walking, swimming, or even mowing the lawn.

Or, you can do 75 minutes a week of vigorous aerobic activity like running or aerobic dancing."

The Mayo Clinic also recommends that you do at least two strength training exercises per week. These could be done using weight machines, going to the gym, rock climbing, heavy gardening, fitness bootcamp, and yoga or pilates classes.

Now is a great time to plan your fitness schedule for the week. How can you dedicate 30 minutes each day to exercise? This short session can be a mixture of a brisk walk, mucking out, going to a keep fit class, or any one of thousands of different sports or exercises you might enjoy.

We've discussed the benefits of yoga—suppleness, balance, relaxation, breath awareness, happiness, confidence, better sleep, greater flexibility, more stamina, and reduced stress. It makes you feel good, and you do it at home or when travelling.

The benefits of yoga, however, are more far-reaching, including greater peace of mind, improved focus and concentration, increased lung capacity, increased metabolism, improved digestion, a 35% increase in flexibility after eight weeks of practice, less chance of heart disease, and better posture.

You can start today by accessing video #1 in the Honest Horse Riding Yoga for Horse Riders Program here: http://www.honesthorseriding.com/bonus

Pilates is another great form of exercise that can help you, in and out of the saddle.

The benefits of pilates include improved flexibility; improved posture; improved physical coordination and balance; relaxation of your shoulders, neck and upper back; increased lung capacity and circulation; improved concentration; better muscle tone and strength; increased body awareness; improved stress management and relaxation.

The difficult part is making the time. But for your health, and your horse riding, it can result in huge benefits.

Chapter 8 assignments

Online exercise

If you haven't accessed these already, download Ozzie's book and video #1 of the Yoga for Horse Riders program here: http://www.honesthorseriding.com/bonus

I'd love to hear your feedback on these in our Facebook community:
https://www.facebook.com/honesthorseriding

Posture exercise

Make a decision to do one form of exercise for 30 minutes every day (not including riding your horse). Your new exercise routine can be anything from a late evening jog to an early morning swim or a lunchtime workout. I find using a pedometer a lot of fun. You can get pedometer apps on your Smartphone, or there are some really nice fitness bands you can get that track all of your steps while you move. My favorites are the Fitbug Orb and the Jawbone Up. They definitely get me moving more every day.

Riding exercise:

As you ride your horse in walk, I want you to focus on your breathing. A clenched ass is something that is quite common in horse riding, so while you are walking around, I want you to imagine that you are breathing out through your ass! This technique may sound a little odd but it really does work to relax all those glutes!

֍֎

Chapter Nine:

Effective communication

"When you're communicating with your horse, it's a private conversation. It's not for everyone to hear."

-Jeff Sanders

Communication between you and your horse is essential to good riding practices. Karen Rohlf from Dressage Naturally said, *"The most important communication is between you and your horse. Many students get stuck because they don't communicate authentically; they interject their or someone else's judgments. The more students trust their instincts about the quality of the communication and remember to let the horse know when he responded as desired, the more effective and harmonious the conversation becomes. It is not just about telling the horse what to do; it is an honest dialogue. The quality of that private communication is more important than what it looks like to anyone else, because that is the only thing the horse cares about."*

Your horse has to understand what you want him to do. Your horse relies on you for guidance. Horsewoman and eventer Janet Patterson explains, *"For me, if you boil it right down, riding is all about communication and balance. [Otherwise], that's just setting you both up to fail."*

You can fine-tune your riding biomechanics even more by implementing three secret methods; they're simple and incredibly effective.

1: Body awareness

Soft fingers

As humans, we develop all sorts of bad habits, for we often use many more muscles than we need to. One example is when we reach for something. Do you move your fingers, or do you move your whole arm? Maybe your whole upper body leans forward, and both your arm and fingers move as well.

Sit at a table that has a few objects on it. Look at something on the table in front of you. It may be a pen or a notebook. First reach for it normally and pick it up. Did you move your upper body?

Now, let's see how little movement you can do to reach and pick it up. First reach forward only with your fingers, very slowly towards the object. Think 'fingers first.' Did you reduce your upper body movement a lot? Did your shoulders stay relaxed, or did they tense up?

Try this exercise a few times each way with different objects on your desk. Your aim is to reach with your fingers first and not to move any part of your body that is not necessary.

Reach for your reins normally. What happens? Now reach for your reins with your fingers first. What happens? While holding reins, do you use your fingers first, or does the whole arm move from the shoulder area?

When you trot, the angle at your elbow will increase to compensate for you rising out of the saddle. If the angle of your elbow stays the same, your hands will rise and fall as your body does, sending unwanted messages to the horse's mouth.

Riding exercise - fingers first:

Sit on your horse at halt. Reach for your reins normally. What happens? Do you tip forwards a little? Do you use extra muscles? Do you do this movement very quickly?

Now let's try it a different way. Very slowly, inch by inch, reach for your reins with the tips of your fingers first. What happens? Is there less movement in your body?

Relaxed shoulders

When we feel tense or stressed, a very common area in our bodies to hold this tension is our shoulders. Becoming more aware of our posture habits in our daily lives is a major breakthrough. For example, I work at a computer a lot, and when I'm knee deep in Excel spreadsheets, the last thing I'm worried about is where my shoulders are. But down the road, if I don't change my habits, carrying tension in my shoulders can easily lead to unwanted back and neck pain and may start to impact other areas of my body.

One thing I do now when I work at a computer is I remind myself every 10 or 15 minutes to breathe out deeply, stare into the distance, and check back in with my body. I imagine my shoulders feeling like melting butter. If I'm leaning forwards, then I rebalance and sit up straight again. If my shoulders are around my ears, I notice them and invite them to lower. Rescuetime.com is a great website to keep track of how many hours you are spending at your computer each day, and to motivate you to reduce this time.

While taking these short breaks was odd in the beginning, I've found it has made a big improvement over the last few months in my own posture. Sometimes I take a break and find I'm actually doing everything right already or just need one or two minor adjustments. Seeing these small improvements will be what drives you to keep improving, and your body will thank you for this.

Riding exercise - shoulders

As you sit on your horse at halt, notice any tension in your shoulders and invite your shoulders to soften and melt, and release that tension. Another really good way to do this is to imagine that your lower arm is really heavy. Having imaginary heavy lower arms will also encourage your shoulders to relax downwards.

Your hands

Your hands should move very little when you ride. Use small cues and be subtle. Riding with one hand is a very effective way to stop moving your hands automatically when you turn, and cut out some bad habits immediately. Hold the reins with one hand and hold the end of the reins with the other hand. Both hands should be in the center of the horse. Do not carry one hand by your side as this body position will cause your body to twist sideways a little. In a safe arena, practice turns at walk while keeping both of your hands near the pommel of the cantle. It might feel a little unusual to begin with! Remember you always want to work on using smaller and more subtle cues. Can you ask your horse to turn by first moving your eyes, then head, then shoulders, then body and legs? Your hands should be one of the last aids you use, not one of the first.

As you pick up the reins, look for the moment your horse softens and rebalances himself. He will feel connected to you and will be listening to see what move you will ask him to do. When he does this, you will feel that you can ask him to move in any direction – forwards, backwards, right or left, with the same ease. In advanced horses it will happen just as you touch the reins. Contact is communication. This is called a soft feel, and is something to work for and it gives remarkable results in your riding.

2: Toes up, heels down

Keeping your heels down is a big issue that a lot of riders want to improve on.

Here is a short and fun exercise you can do while you are sitting in a chair to help you to sit deep in the saddle and to keep your center of gravity nice and low. Once you try this short exercise in a chair a few times, you can practise it with your horse.

- Sit on a chair with your feet flat on the ground.
- Lift your toes upwards
- Are there any changes in the rest of your body?
- Now put your feet flat on the ground again.
- Push your heels down into the ground.
- What happens to your body?

You will have noticed that your whole body lifts up out of the seat, when you push your heels into the ground. This result is not good when you ride because you do not want to be pushing yourself up and out of the saddle.

The next time you ride, focus for five minutes on pointing your toes up, instead of pushing your heels down and see how this affects your riding and position.

Saddle exercise – stirrup focus

Remember, you want to push weight off of your stirrups, not from your thighs. Here is an exercise to do without your horse:

- Stand still facing someone else. Think about something else and relax. Ask your friend to very gently push your collarbone, which should cause you to lean back a little.

- Stand still facing someone and focus on your stomach. Ask your friend to very gently push your collarbone, which should cause you to lean back a little.

- Stand still facing someone and focus on having your weight in your feet. Ask your friend to very gently push your collarbone, which should cause you to lean back a little.

• In which of these three experiments did you move the most? In which of these three experiments did you move the least? Was it what you had expected? (Often it isn't!)

ଞ୍ଚଔ

Chapter 9 assignments

Online exercise

Start to track your daily progress in the My Horse Riding Makeover app. Updating the iPhone app will take about three minutes each day, and it's a great way to track your improvements.

Posture exercise

While you are at work, I want you to concentrate this week on releasing the tension in your shoulders every hour or more often if you can remember to do this. Releasing tension is a great habit to get used to and will absolutely help your riding.

Riding exercise

Your goal when riding this week is to move your hands and arms very little. Instead, I want you to think of using only your fingers   first and seeing how little movement can produce great results from your horse. Often, the less you do, the more you get.

৪০৫৪

Chapter 10:

Advanced rider biomechanics

"If you want your horse to follow your focus then you had better know what you are focusing on. This can be as simple as just riding to a point in the arena or on the trail or as complex as knowing what plan you are working on. Having focus or a plan gives us great leadership; in the absence of a plan your horse will make his own. "

--Sarah Brady

The magic with horses happens when both of you are listening and connecting mentally with each other. But there are lots of situations where this connection doesn't happen.

- The horse is distracted and looking outwards and his mind is two miles away. It happened to me in 2014 at a clinic. My first lesson was a mess! I wasn't breathing, I was very nervous, and I offered no solutions to help my horse. The trainer kindly suggested that I work some simple serpentines. After a few minutes, with my attention now back on my horse and a plan in place, both of us started to relax and look a lot more calm.

- The rider is distracted. Maybe you're thinking of a horrible manager at work, what's for dinner, what is on

TV tonight, or chatting to a friend. The rider is not 'present.' I've been guilty of being distracted in the past. I expected my horse to be listening to me, but sometimes I ignored him.

- The rider has a certain level of awareness, but does not yet realize there is so much more available. Focusing more on the present and analyzing each muscle movement and communication from the horse can open up communication lines that are so clear it's like you are both speaking the same language. Working by becoming more aware of your own body and working on living in the moment are great ways to start this journey.

Engaging your body all the time

Like horses and other animals, your body should always be ready to go somewhere. Don't switch off and dump your weight on the floor. Your whole body should feel active even when you are not moving. You should feel as if you are about to move.

No jerky movements

Slowly and gently, bring your arm up to your hair. Smooth a little of your hair, and then slowly and gently bring your arm back down again to your side.

Thoughtful body movements are probably something we don't normally do. Instead, we swipe back our hair, and instead of slowly bringing our arms back down to our sides, we allow them to drop down with gravity very quickly, and they crash to our sides.

This jerky movement is not good, for it actually disengages your body and affects your breathing, your eyesight blurs for a second, and it can take between 5 and 30 seconds for you to rebalance again after that jerky arm movement.

If you turn on the TV or touch something, focus on bringing it back down slowly again. No jerky movements. Think of everything as being like a dance.

If you throw a ball with your arm, that arm doesn't crash to your side. Instead, it lowers slowly.

- No 100% fast releases. Be more present with your whole body. Remember to move your limbs gently and thoughtfully. When your limbs move fast, your breathing can get interrupted for a second or two, with the same effect in your eyesight comprehension.

Pay more attention to your arms, hands, and feet and place them gently and slowly instead of letting gravity crash them down.

Mindful riding

Always gently and softly get on and off your horse. It's best to use a mounting block. Over time, mounting from the ground puts a lot of extra unwanted pressure on one side of your horse. You don't want to do something that can cause issues in a few years.

Be gentle with your weight movement. If you are digging your seat bones into your horse's back or slamming down on his back when you do rising trot, your weight is all going to cause him pain. This unbalanced and sudden weight pressure can lead to a tight and hollow back and an annoyed horse.

Riding exercise: A really good exercise while you ride is to see how light your horse's footfalls can get. Listen to the footfall, and try and be really quiet so you feel like you are riding on very delicate egg shells, and you are not allowed to break them.

Sitting trot

Sitting trot is something that many riders have difficulty with. First, focus on releasing extra tension from your body. Are your glutes clenched? Invite them to unclench; otherwise, sitting trot will be quite difficult.

Work on identifying and releasing any other tension in your body, including in your shoulders, and do this in walk first before you think about sitting trot.

Now focus on your breathing. Pause after you breathe out and allow your diaphragm to power your breathing.

Your horse's spine moves right and left, so allow your lower body to move right and left. This experience feels the same as riding down steep hills. Your horse also moves right and left in trot. Your body also goes right and left in trot.

Many top dressage riders don't follow this movement; instead they go up and down. This upwards/downwards movement blocks the horse's hind leg and impedes the horse's movement. In sitting trot, think about your lower body going right and left. When you can't keep up to the rhythm any more in sitting trot, go to rising trot.

Transitions

Before you trot, you should think about having a walk full of energy that feels like it is on the verge of trotting. When a horse is prepared, it takes very little (sometimes just a thought), to move him into a trot. But a horse that isn't prepared, that is perhaps walking very slowly with no energy, looking outside the arena, and is mentally not with you, is a lot trickier. The key is to get into the horse's mind and to have him mentally with you. Then, the manoeuvres become much easier.

Exhale on transitions

Remember, upward transitions start with the horse's hindquarters, so visualize these in your mind as the powerhouse where the trot will begin. You must honestly want the horse to trot, so think forward and allow a little room in the reins for the horse to move on. If you are scared or nervous, it's common to think you are applying the 'trot' cues - but in reality, your body is screaming to the horse that you do not want him to go a fraction faster than the walk speed he is currently at.

When you are trotting, push your weight from the stirrups so you can keep the rest of your legs, thighs, and glutes relaxed. Focus on sitting very lightly each time your seat comes back to the saddle. Remember the broken eggs?

The art of not talking (hush-hush!)

Simply put, try not to talk when you ride and see what happens. When I am not talking, I find it's much easier to feel my horse's movement. It's also much easier to smile and easier to listen to your horse a lot more. Not speaking while you ride sounds simple on paper, but it can make a HUGE change in your riding. It's a great exercise to try the next time you are riding.

Intent and honesty

Intent and honesty are very important to bear in mind when we ride our horses. Horses are 100% honest. They communicate what they think. They don't lie, they don't pretend to be someone they are not, and they don't say one thing and mean another.

They expect the same from us. We can run into difficulties when our intent doesn't match our actions (which our horses can understand perfectly). Conscious and unconscious dishonesty can negatively impact our riding.

Imagine you want your horse to canter. You're applying your normal cues, but inside of you, you are scared that your horse might be overexcited and buck or take off. Your intent, therefore, is really for your horse to stay trotting. Your horse knows your intent because your body is also communicating this to him, through tension and how tightly you are gripping the reins.

There are lots of other examples as well. When you are riding, ask yourself if your intent truly matches what you are asking your horse to do.

How to keep improving

Here's a simple way you can always keep improving your technique. I call it the "photo shoot" method.

Ask someone to take five pictures on their phone of you riding. Look at them and pick out the two habits you'd most like to fix.

For the next five days, focus on improving only two bad habits. It's a really great way to focus. After five days, get someone to take another five pictures and see the improvements.

Improvement is a daily process, but with dedication and commitment, you will see results.

As master equine artist Tony O'Connor beautifully summarized, *"Everything isn't always simply black or white. The darkness of my canvases and the emergence of the horse symbolizes that no matter how dark, how bleak and how empty things may seem, beauty, power and strength can prevail."*

By improving ourselves we are creating beauty in our horsemanship.

৪৩৫৪

Chapter 10 assignments

Online exercise

Do you need more help? Every few months, we open up our five week online Honest Horse Riding course to new participants. It's designed to help you to change small, practical things in your daily life which can result in big improvements in the quality of your horse riding. Today's exercise is to visit: http://www.honesthorseriding.com/online-course/ and see if this course is something that you feel would be beneficial to you.

Posture exercise

This week when you are at home or at work, I want you to focus on being more aware of how you move your legs, feet, and arms and try to do less automatic jerky movements. Instead, move your arms and legs slowly and feel the difference in your body.

Riding exercise

As you ride this week, I want you to start listening to your horse's footfalls. Now it's your job to make them quieter. Explore what you can do to make this change.

෩෬

Afterword

I truly hope you've enjoyed this book and are already beginning to implement some of the techniques we've covered to improve your riding and your overall quality of life.

You've made a huge step towards finding more balance in every aspect of your life. I'm incredibly proud of you!

The lessons I've shared are straight-forward to implement, but you have to be willing to try them! Be the 1% of people who read this book and take action. Consistency is key to any kind of self-improvement, whether you're cultivating a regular yoga practice, or riding horses. Action is what counts.

Be sure to utilize all of the special bonuses I've created for you at http://www.honesthorseriding.com/bonus. They'll give you extra support and help keep you moving forward, in and out of the saddle!

If you have received value from this book, I would be very grateful if you could leave a book review on Amazon. Book reviews are really important for authors, for they help other people looking for ways to improve their horse riding to find this book on Amazon.

If you are looking for some inspiration and advice to improve your horsemanship and partnership with your horse, the finest book I have read on this topic is 'True Horsemanship through Feel', by Bill Dorrance. It is a very enjoyable book to read, with stories and photos throughout the book. Bill Dorrance is regarded as one of the most phenomenal horse men in the world. I would highly recommend this book to you. It is one of my absolute favorites and a goldmine of useful information to get along better with your horse.

Finally, I'd love to know what your 'aha!' moments were while reading this book. Join our Facebook community and let me know your biggest takeaways and what you're going to work on this week with your horse.

Facebook community:
https://www.facebook.com/honesthorseriding

To your horse riding success and happiness,
Elaine Heney
www.honesthorseriding.com

Resources, Thanks & Valued Contributors

Thank you to the wonderful Honest Horse Riding community, especially my wonderful editors and proof readers: Lesley Laurence, Michelle Edge, Chris Wolf, Gemma Hague, Ruth Sonke, Marie-Jeanne Ribbink, Valerie Leonard and Carmel O'Callaghan. Thank you also to the many friends and colleagues who kindly contributed their thoughts to this book. You can read more details about their work below.

Amanda Barton

Amanda Barton is an equine expert and trainer. She has a postgraduate diploma in animal behavior and is a qualified NLP practitioner and qualified equine sports massage therapist. Amanda's particular specialism is quality foundation training for horses of all ages both from the ground or ridden. Amanda's goal is to help each horse and rider to find softness, symmetry and connection so that they can work together harmoniously. She has studied with a wide range of trainers all over the world in a quest to find effective ways to work with horses softly and with connection. To learn more about Amanda, please visit www.amandabarton.com

Peter Bennett

Peter is a Chartered Physiotherapist and is registered with the Health Professionals Council. He is a specialist in treating musculoskeletal dysfunction, including neck, back and knee problems, and sports injuries using soft tissue techniques and 'hands on' skills along with electrotherapy and ultrasound treatment. To learn more about Peter, please visit www.penrithchiropractic.com

Sarah Brady

Sarah and Chris Brady have been involved in the Parelli Programme since it was first launched in Ireland in 2007. They both study internationally with some of the best horsemen and are dedicated in helping people achieve their dreams with horses. Learn more at www.parelli-instructors-Ireland.com

Isabell Brenner

Isabell Brenner is an equine expert and owner of the Silversand Horsemanship clinic in Germany. In her own words, "It is very important to me, through communication, to create a partnership with the horse to develop as the foundation for everything. I want the horse to understand and be ready, and to have no fear. In this way it is possible to discover the great potential in every horse and achieve exceptional performances." To learn more about Isabell, please visit http://www.horsemanship-brenner.de/

Lisa Bruin

Lisa has spent her life working with horses; she has travelled worldwide working and training with some of the world's top horsemen. Lisa's aim, through her teaching, is to provide the horse owner with knowledge of not only how to produce good quality safe riding horses, but also how to move them on to performance level. She holds clinics throughout the year in UK and Europe. To learn more about Lisa, please visit www.lisabruin.com

Kas Fitzpatrick

Kas Fitzpatrick is the founder of Exploring Horsemanship. Over the last 12 years she has been the clinic organizer for Steve Halfpenny, Tom Widdicombe, Amanda Barton, Dave Stuart, and various Parelli Natural

Horsemanship instructors at different times. She lives in the UK with her beloved horses, Celebrity Psyche, Tee Pee, and Fin. To learn more, please visit

www.exploringhorsemanship.com

Cathy Johns

Cathy Johns is a horsewoman from New Zealand. She is the Chief Trek Guide for the popular Mt. Lyford horse treks. Her philosophy is helping people to help their horses. She doesn't call herself a horse trainer because training people brings the best result from their horses.

Ben Moxon

Ben teaches horsemanship in the UK. Ben believes in the idea of horsemanship as an art in which you can keep developing and growing as time goes by. Ben sees this as different from riding (although riding is an important part of it) because it encompasses all parts of the way you are with horses. What Ben has learned comes from the tradition of trainers, such as Bill and Tom Dorrance, and Ray Hunt, as practised by modern trainers, such as Buck Brannaman and Martin Black. To learn more, please visit : www.pragmatichorsemanship.co.uk

Tony O'Connor

With a disciplined approach to his study of horse anatomy, Tony puts great emphasis on technical execution. As with much of his work, the void of background and simplicity of the pieces serve to highlight the natural physical perfection of these animals. The horse and the beauty of its majestic form and spirit are the basis of his canvas. The result of his inimitable combination of an innate aptitude for draughtsmanship and his lifelong passion for horses is a body of beautifully evocative paintings that capture the unique power, grace and nobility of the equine form. Discover more at www.whitetreestudio.ie

Maria O'Neill

Maria is an Alexander Technique instructor in Ireland. In her own words, "As a horse rider all my life, finding the Alexander Technique in my 40's brought new insights to the world of the equine for me. It has expanded my life in general and brought improvements to my health which have allowed me to continue to enjoy many of the things I most like to do. As I teacher I am privileged to pass on some of that knowledge and its benefits to other riders at all levels." To learn more, please visit balanceinaction@mariaoneill.ie

Maria O'Rourke

Maria began her career in human dentistry in 1992 and then went on to combine her passion for horses with her professional career to qualify as an equine dentist. These days domestic horses suffer from many problems such as poor tooth alignment and irregular chewing patterns that can cause severe pain, digestive difficulty, colic, and behavioural and performance problems. Maria works in Ireland. To learn more about Maria, please visit:
www.Equinedentist.ie

Dr. Nikki Osborne

Dr. Nikki Osborne is a widely-respected physician in London, England. She has held the position of Senior Scientific Officer at the Royal Society for the Prevention of Cruelty to Animals since 2005. Dr. Osborne holds a PhD in Neurology and a BSc in Neuroscience. She has been a vocal advocate for animal protection, presenting at multiple global conferences. Her work is published in multiple peer-reviewed journals, including the American Journal of Bioethics, Lab Animal Europe, Animal Technology and Welfare and Nature Cell Biology.

Janet Patterson

Janet is an event rider who has made a point of studying all aspects of horsemanship. She is also fortunate enough to have been chosen to be one of only 16 students on the teachers' training program with international dressage master Philippe Karl. To learn more, please visit: www.babelhorse.com

Karen Rohlf

Karen Rohlf has been helping transform students' connection with their horses for 30 years. Her background is in competitive dressage, training for over 20 years with International competitor and FEI 5* Judge Anne Gribbons. This, coupled with her study of natural horsemanship, gives her a unique perspective. She is the creator of an educational system for horses and riders called Dressage, Naturally. Her holistic approach to training empowers students to create stronger partnerships and healthy biomechanics, so riders can enjoy more results in harmony with their horses! She is a *pioneer of independent learning programs for riders. To learn more, please visit: dressagenaturally.net.*

Johannes Stübben

Johannes Stübben is a manager at Stübben Saddles in Germany. He hails from one of the most respected names in saddles and is a direct descendent of Johannes Willhem Stübben, the founder of Stübben Saddles. Stübben Saddles are the world's premiere brand of saddles respected and revered worldwide. Founded in 1894, the brand has stood for quality, craftsmanship, and unparalleled excellence for over 100 years. As a specialist family enterprise that provides exclusive riding equipment, Stübben perfectly combines traditional craftsmanship with modern functionality. Stübben products are a truly global brand, available in more than 50 countries and on all five continents. The family business can now look back on a success story of more than 120 years. For more information about the company, please visit:

http://www.stuebben.com/index_com.php

Tom Widdicombe

Tom Widdicombe has worked with his own and other people's horses for over 30 years. With his wife Sarah, he has run successful clinics throughout the UK and Ireland. He is the author of two well-received books on horsemanship.

Tom's latest book is available at:
http://www.amazon.co.uk/Baucher-Ordinary-Horseman-Tom-Widdicombe-ebook/dp/B00MMM43HA

To learn more about Tom, please visit:
http://www.tomwiddicombe.com

My Horse Riding Makeover iPhone iPad app:

Download the app at:
https://itunes.apple.com/app/my-horse-riding-makeover-fix/id931210190?mt=8

My Horse Riding Makeover 5 week online course:

Get on the 5 week online 'My Horse Riding Makeover' waiting list here: http://www.honesthorseriding.com/online-course/

೫೦೮೩

CPSIA information can be obtained
at www.ICGtesting.com
Printed in the USA
BVHW040158070819
555291BV00015B/155/P